STRAIGHT TALK IS MORE THAN WORDS

STRAIGHT TALK IS MORE THAN WORDS

Persuasive Communications:
The Key to Achieving Your Goals

Patricia Ann Ball

STRAIGHT TALK IS MORE THAN WORDS
Persuasive Communications: The Key to Achieving Your Goals

Trudy Knox, Publisher
168 Wildwood Drive
Granville, OH 43023-1073

Sue Politella, Editor
Orrville, OH

Wendy Kuhn, Illustrator
St. Louis, MO

First Edition

ISBN: 1-887373-00-4
LC: 95-082256

CONTENTS

Foreword

Patricia Ann Ball is right on target when she points out how empowering it is to realize that we constantly have choices to make about our actions and response to situations. Once we sense this power, understanding that it is private and inviolable, and that it grows as we grow, we release ourselves from the miscommunication and fear of expressing ourselves that intimidate so many. We learn early in *Straight Talk Is More Than Words* that the power of choice is ours. We can give it up, but it can never be taken from us without our consent.

Ball goes on to show how this intrinsic power is related to communication and persuasion in many forms, from the most obvious — words — to the often more telling nonverbal behavior. She steps us through all the components we use, some knowingly, some reflexively. She takes us to the heart of the matter — the response from our audience, whether that audience is your life partner, a child, 50 potential clients or 10,000 diverse humans who share at least one reason for being in the same place at the same time as you.

With her twenty years as a professional actor in live theater, Ball sees and clearly explains the spectrum of techniques at our disposal for "setting the stage" for our message — from when and how to use humor; what difference gender makes and when it makes none at all; why power is related to the response you achieve; when brevity and silence are better than words; how to use the space around you as effectively as eye contact, a handshake, a smile and body language. And don't forget listening, a critical skill good talkers often ignore.

Straight Talk Is More Than Words is a book about communication and personal power. We learn how to communicate better in order to achieve understanding. After all, getting ourselves understood is the first step in getting what we want in the more tangible sense — a promotion, a lower price on a dream house, commitment from a store clerk to correct a mistake, a standing ovation from an audience which listened intently, and on and on throughout life.

Jim Tunney, Ed.D., CSP, CPAE
Professional Speaker and Former NFL Referee
Pebble Beach, California

To my husband, Ken Ball, Ph.D.,
my best friend, colleague, confidant and lover.
To my dad, Oris R. Whitley,
who always told me I could accomplish
whatever I chose to do.
To my children, David and Dana,
whose existence has enriched my life ten-fold.

Introduction

All the World's a Stage
And all the men and women merely players;
They have their exits and their entrances;
And one man in his time plays many parts.
As You Like It
\- William Shakespeare

As always, William Shakespeare gets to the heart of the matter. All the world certainly is a stage, and you — the salesperson, the manager, the every man/woman — are also an actor, playing many roles throughout the day. When you go to a job interview, you show your best side — the picture of success. In your office setting you are a friendly, competent colleague. At home you are the loving parent or spouse. How you play your roles will determine your ability to influence others and, ultimately, to succeed.

My background includes not only twenty years as a communications specialist, but also years as a professional actor. I think it will be fun to treat this book as if it were a play. You'll learn not only to play the part, but also, through visualization, to get into the mind of your hearer. The theater/stage illustrates the power of communication bringing the listeners into the hearts of the players. Just as the audience is swept into the drama on stage, in like manner the players relate to the hearers and respond to their expectations.

If you want to rise to the top of your profession and make more *money*, the *proven* techniques in this book are *guaranteed* to get *results*. Many of the steps are *easy* to incorporate into your daily life. They will *save* you from making some common mistakes along the way.

Included in this book are some *new* ideas as well as older *proven*, *safe* methods of communicating that will *free* you from ineffective habits you may have developed. In your quest for *health*, happiness and the American Dream for yourself and the ones you love, the *choice* to become more persuasive and convincing and therefore more powerful is yours to make.

I wrote the last two paragraphs to demonstrate the power of persuasive language, to have a little fun and to give you a sample of what you can learn from this book. According to a study at Yale University, the words in italics in the two paragraphs are the most persuasive in the English language. I choose to add *choice* to this list. The fact that you have a choice in everything you do is self-empowering.

Power words are just the beginning. The word "communication" has many meanings.

- Expressing yourself so others understand you is the basic level of communication. If your message is interesting enough that your hearers stay with you voluntarily instead of wandering off mentally, that is good communication.

- If your presentation motivates your hearers to act on your idea, that's a good first move toward power. Motivation is not enough by itself, though. The world is full of people who were fired up but who ran out of fuel the next day.

- Showing how to get started is another step. The highest level of power communication is to empower your hearers to make changes.

Straight Talk Is More Than Words includes information which will help you to be more convincing in your words and in your behavior. My experience in the corporate world and as a consultant and professional speaker has taught me that straight talk is a great deal more than words.

Communication is more than what you say and show by your nonverbal expression; it is also how your hearers respond. What response do you want? How can you get it? To create the response you want in your audience, you need to know your listeners' needs. Your desired responses may be the same for different audiences, but your methods must be as different as the group's needs are. If you plan your conversations instead of blurting out whatever is on the top of your head, you are already on the road to power.

* * * * * *

This book will teach you straight talk techniques to use in situations that require you to be convincing and persuasive.

- First we set the stage and explore the theme of *Straight Talk Is More Than Words*. Straight talk means power communications. We examine the various meanings of the words "power" and "communication." Here we introduce the straight talk tools you must develop internally so that the external tools will work.

- Next we'll deal with the "read-through" or character development stages of an actor's life. In an actual play, this stage of rehearsal is spent learning the psychological nature of the character you are to play. You will learn to understand yourself. You'll explore the personal tools of power — those behaviors that make you more powerful in general. This segment also covers self-esteem, confidence and self-worth.

- Then we'll learn how to shape your "character" to play your role as a straight talker more effectively. We will examine the powerful person's communications tools which relate to behavior — listening skills, gender communication skills and humor. Then we'll look at the verbal and nonverbal external tools of power communications. We will explore direct speech, brevity of speech, cerebral speech, the use of silence and the speech of "positive intent." We'll cover powerless verbal behaviors, including qualifiers and empty superlatives. The section on nonverbal tools of the powerful covers paralanguage, posture, height, gestures, handshakes, facial expressions and use of space. Just as an actor must master these techniques to convincingly portray a character, we must do the same to effectively play our life role.

- We examine various life stage settings. In theater, there are *proscenium settings, thrust stages* and *theaters-in-the-round.* Each of these stage settings requires different directorial approaches. The stage of life is filled with similarly unique stage settings which require special communication techniques. We'll explore powerful methods for conducting meetings. We'll examine conflict situations and ways to deal with them. We'll look at ways to enhance a presentation.

- The "dress rehearsal" is an examination of how we can enhance our communication skills by "costuming" correctly for the role. This portion investigates the subtleties that create the visual aspect of our "character." In addition to looking at overall image factors, it explores the actual costume itself — the various ways that our dress communicates.
- Finally everything comes together on Opening Night which summarizes where you are going and how you will get there. If you carefully follow all the steps to this point, you will become a successful straight talker.

1
Power and Communication

In a play, before any action can take place, the play's setting has to be planned. The stage for the action has to be set. The same is true of understanding communications. We must begin with some basic premises.

In today's fast-paced world of business, if there's anything we have in abundance, it's communication. Unfortunately, much of this is inept or inaccurate communication — or just noise. It doesn't provide any real information. Each of the above descriptions of the communication process — inept or inaccurate communication or noise — has special meaning. The following story bandied about by communication specialists is a humorous demonstration of *inept* communication.

A woman goes to her lawyer and says, "I need a divorce." "Okay," answers the lawyer, "do you have grounds?" "Why, yes. An acre and a half." "No, do you have a grudge?" "No, but we have a carport." "Does your husband beat you up?" "No, I get up way before he does." "Madam, do you really want a divorce?" "No, it's my husband who wants the divorce. He has trouble communicating with me."

Inaccurate communication occurs when one party fails to express in a clear, understandable way what she means to another party. The most frustrating experience I have had with miscommunication occurred many years ago during one of my first radio commercial recording sessions. The director for the commercial instructed me to sound "bitchy, sexy." I did not understand what he meant. In retake after retake after retake, I sounded either too bitchy or too sexy. He then asked me to sound like a radio personality that *he* knew but whom *I* had never heard! After twenty retakes he finally said, "Let's just forget it," and dismissed me. Since that occasion there have been numerous soap opera characters with whom I could have identified, but at that time I didn't have a clue. This was an example of *inaccurate* communication! The director was unable to accurately describe to me exactly how he wanted me to sound.

Noise has specific meanings in the context of communication. There are two kinds of communication noise — physical and psychological. Physical noise has to do with physical things that interfere with the communications process. If you are in a crowded room and many people are talking at once, this is physical noise. But it can also be a room filled with so much smoke that you are distracted from hearing what is being said. Perhaps you are seated in the back of a large auditorium and the sound system doesn't carry to your seat. Anything that affects your ability to hear is physical noise.

Psychological noise has no material form; it comes from within ourselves. Perhaps we are listening through stereo-types. Our perception of what is being discussed may be vastly different from the other person's. Perhaps they are using jargon or psycho-babble that we don't understand.

Use straight talk to develop your communicative powers and overcome many communication mishaps. *Straight talk* will help you stand out from the background of dismal communi-cation.

When you speak, you want people to remember what you say. To be effective in straight talk in today's world and in the future, it is necessary:

- to be a good listener and questioner
- to be sensitive to the needs of others
- to sense the unspoken
- to listen more than talk
- to know body language and adapt that knowledge to yourself as well as read it in others
- to be knowledgeable about your field, products and/or services

The first five of these requirements illustrate the importance of listening skills. Communication is a two-way street. It doesn't do any good to speak of your field, products or services unless you can reach your audience. Listening to others requires more work than presenting your own case, but the end results are most rewarding.

Because the future is **now**, today's business people need to be tremendously sophisticated. Our new information society is the most rapidly-changing environment in history. Coping with change is our number-one priority. First and foremost, a straight talker needs to be a change agent.

To be an effective change agent in today's fast-moving world, you need a number of straight talking attributes. We often think of charisma as one attribute of the straight talker, but it is not the only one. The straight talking power communicator must also be informed, authoritative and persuasive.

The word "power" has both positive and negative connotations. Power over yourself is a valuable tool. When a powerful person tells herself to do something, she does it at the right time and in the right way. There is no procrastination and no short cut. When you are in charge of yourself, you will also be in charge of your communications.

Power over others may suggest manipulation and control, intimidation and dominance; and these are ideas which bother many people. Throughout this book all references are to positive power — using power to help others become empowered. People give more if empowered than if intimidated. People who use intimidation to control other people feel powerless and vulnerable underneath, and the results are often negative. This dictatorial behavior is akin to the out-of-control behavior you see in a small child having a tantrum.

If you say to an employee, "Do as I say," you might achieve your goal. People will sometimes grudgingly knuckle under. But what will be the end result? What happens when people are forced to do what you want by use of intimidation? How will they behave?

They might slow down a little in the work process, or maybe they will do only what is expected of them, putting forth no extra effort. Perhaps they will display a negative attitude. In some way they will defy you even if their defiance isn't obvious.

Using a manipulative method in a sales situation might make a sale, but could well lose that customer's business — a negative result in the long term. Building lasting relationships is a primary goal in business. Manipulative tactics can backfire and destroy the relationship — another negative result. So when I use the word "power," I mean positive power, which builds rather than destroys. Power is persuasive communications.

Reflect on the meaning of power and communication. One dictionary defines power as "the ability to effect change, to mobilize resources, to persuade or influence others toward a goal." Some equate power with control. When I say "power," I mean self-control, the ability to control your own behavior. You can manage your own behavior in such a way that others will change their behaviors as a result. Being comfortable with power, you can then help others empower themselves.

A dictionary definition of communication is "expressing yourself clearly with the words and nonverbal behavior being congruent in reflecting your intention." For example, if your intention is to be friendly, then your words and body language will both convey that same message of friendship. If your intention is only an intellectual and not an emotional one, your body will send out a different signal, confusing the hearers. Insincerity will negate whatever idea you are trying to convey.

Real power comes from within. It is an attitude, not a series of words. It encompasses the development of a number of behavioral skills. Being persistent, having a vision, looking to the future, being knowledge-oriented and a risk taker, having a consistently positive attitude and learning to be assertive are all internal positive behaviors of the straight talker.

2
The Power That Comes From Within

Behaviors which empower others come from within. You need to achieve them to be effective in your chosen role in life, just as an actor needs internal behaviors to portray a character. Strength, energy and belief in yourself come from within.

If you develop the internal tools of power, the external tools will follow. Actors are taught that everything flows from inside to outside. If the actor doesn't believe in the character, how can she convince the audience? Most powerful people have the following seven internal behavior styles, which I call the Powers from Within:

- persistence
- visionary goal-setting
- orientation toward the future
- orientation toward learning and knowledge
- innovative risk-taking
- a positive attitude
- assertive behavior

You strengthen your message when you communicate clearly and deliberately and have an end goal for your conversation rather than simply talking aimlessly. Have you ever said anything that made you think to yourself, "I can't believe I said that?" If so, then you were speaking off the top of your head with no set goal for the communication.

Only recently I pulled such a personal boner. At a meeting I was asked to stand and state my name and occupation. As CEO of my own company, Patricia Ball Corporate Communications, I have drafted many of my own ads and written some of my own publicity. Over the years I have written the term "nationally acclaimed speaker" hundreds of times. I stood up at the meeting and said, "Hello, I'm Patricia Ball. I'm a nationally acclaimed speaker." Ugh! What I meant to say was, "I'm a national speaker." The attendees must have thought I was terribly conceited. The problem was unplanned communication — just talk — with no end goal.

Power communication requires clarity, precision, authority and congruence. For clarity of speech, you need to ensure that what you are saying has the same meaning to your listener as it does to you. One useful way to check this is to get feedback from your listener. Ask, "Was I making myself clear?" or "To be sure that I've made myself clear, could you repeat in your own words what you believe I said?"

Precision in your speech is another important pointer for becoming a straight talker. Powerful communicators will go to great lengths to find the perfect word to fit a situation — the word that has the exact nuance needed. Carefully select the word or phrase that most definitively describes what you mean.

For authority in your speech, use words that carry strength like "excellence" and "magnificent." Rather than indirectly approaching a point, be direct. Be brief. Avoid extraneous words and qualifying phrases like "It's only my opinion."

Power speakers must also be verbally and bodily congruent. They must think consciously and have in mind the results they want. Your body should convey the same message as your words. If you have conflicting intentions, your body will leak tell-tale signals and sabotage you. When words and bodies send different messages, people believe the body rather than the words. For example, if I say, "I'm pleased to meet you," but my arms are crossed on my chest, I have no smile and my brow is furrowed, would you believe that I am really pleased to meet you? You can tell a lot about people by reading them nonverbally. Body language is the most honest form of communication we can use.

When you become more aware of your own body language, you will understand yourself better and your communication skills will increase. Straight talkers begin with a thorough understanding of themselves in order to understand others.

Your biases, prejudices and predispositions are communications filters. If you are unaware of the components of those filters, you may give off unintended signals. The greater the extent to which an individual understands himself, the more likely the talk will be straight to the intended target.

3
Understanding Self

Life is like a play in which one is cast to play a role. An actor's success depends upon how well she communicates a role to the audience. So does yours. Your success is directly related to how well you understand the people with whom you come in daily contact and how well they understand you.

An actor's concerns in communicating the playwright's meaning are the same as your concerns in dealing with people. Communicating is much more than words alone. It is how the words are said, when they are said, how they are meant and how they are interpreted. It is the expression on your face; it is even in silences. Many of the skills you need to function powerfully in the world of work are the same skills an actor develops in the world of theater.

To act effectively you must learn to understand yourself, to understand others and, finally, to use the tools that allow you to communicate this understanding to the audience: body language, voice and intonations. Effective managers must do the same. The tools that actors use to communicate the essence of the characters they depict are extremely useful in your own daily encounters with people.

In theater, after the selection process is completed and the play is cast, the director schedules rehearsals. Preliminary rehearsals or "read-throughs" are designed to help the actor get in touch with himself and to understand the character he is to play. Before you embark on the stage of life, you also need to understand your character — yourself — and your weaknesses, strengths and blind spots. You must understand yourself before you can understand others, because you need to recognize your own personal blind spots. We all have them. Knowing yours will give you more power.

One major barrier to understanding others is the inability to be honest with ourselves. Carl Rogers, a noted psychologist, is reported to have said that he can only be helpful to another person if he can permit himself to understand that person. He then pointed out the significance of the word "permit." Whoever undertakes to genuinely understand another runs a risk of being changed in the process. The illustration titled **SELF-IMAGES** is a diagram of the depth of understanding an actor must reach to successfully play a character. Using this as a life metaphor, you need to go through a similar process to reach full understanding of your own self-image.

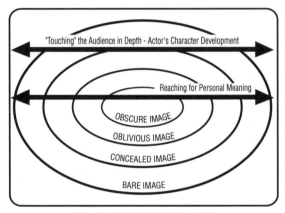

Touching" the Audience in Depth - Actor's Character Development

Reaching for Personal Meaning

OBSCURE IMAGE

OBLIVIOUS IMAGE

CONCEALED IMAGE

BARE IMAGE

SELF-IMAGES

The same principles can be applied to your audience — the people with whom you come in contact. As the ovals in the diagram widen, the actor gets deeper and deeper into character development. She also digs deeper and deeper into self-understanding and, as a result, is able to touch, involve or sell the audience.

Let's briefly define these self-images:

1. First, there is the bare image or the common area, a part of us known both to us and to any other observers of the open area of an interrelationship.

2. Our concealed image is that part of us which we hide from others: our very private world, our insecurities. These are the attitudes, feelings and values of which we are aware but do not reveal to others.

3. Our oblivious image is that part which is unknown to us but that others can see. This image contains those things we *could* see and even understand if we would just allow ourselves to do so, such as our fears and prejudices.

4. Our obscure image has to do with the things that motivate us which we don't understand. This image is obscure both to us and to others. It includes that mysterious something deep inside which starts our knees knocking, stomach churning or voice squeaking when we have to talk to someone in authority. The failure to understand ourselves is an obstacle to self-knowledge, presenting a challenge that few of us meet.

If we can close the gap between what we know about ourselves and what others know, and if we can increase the common area known by both, then our communications will be much more effective. This increase in communication efficiency is one of the major benefits of gaining insight into our own emotional responses.

Another significant barrier to understanding others is stereotyping — but not just the stereotypes we're familiar with through public opinion and legislation. These stereotypes may actually be easier to deal with on an individual level than the attitudes, feelings and beliefs that are deep inside each one of us. We all have "tapes" in our heads that repeat negative generalities we've heard throughout our life. No one likes to admit to stereotyping. It doesn't sound politically or socially correct. Yet we all do it on one level or another. The misconceptions which we commonly acquire at the earliest stages of awareness and understanding become a basic part of our personalities. They inhibit honest, open communication, causing us to hear from others only what we expect to hear and to see in others only what we expect to see.

Whether we are trying to persuade one person or a thousand, we must force ourselves to see past the stereotypes we've built in our minds. We must master our blind spots so that we do not project our feelings and self-images onto others. That is the challenge.

4
Internal Power Tools

Just as actors need to understand the internal workings or motivations of the characters they are portraying, we need to understand ourselves as the first step toward developing a solid sense of our "role in life." Since self-understanding comes from within, the next step is to discover within ourselves the internal behaviors that most successful people possess. These behaviors are persistence, visionary goal-setting, orientation toward the future, orientation toward learning and knowledge, innovative risk-taking, having a positive attitude and using assertive behavior.

Persistence

Persistence is found in powerful leaders. These people are extremely focused. They do not waver from their ultimate purpose and their set of personal values and goals. For example, when President Reagan told flight controllers if they did not return to work the next day they would be fired and not rehired, he followed through and his persistence added to his credibility. When President Kennedy faced the Cuban missile crisis, most believed that he would follow through with his stated purpose and not waver. Whether you agreed or disagreed with these men, you still knew that you could count on what they promised if it was at all in their power to deliver. If you have such determination, your customers and colleagues will know that if you promise delivery by a certain deadline, you will move heaven and earth to meet that deadline.

Thomas Edison committed himself to discovering a filament that would turn bright white in a vacuum when electricity passed through it. He experimented with approximately 6,000 different materials before he tried tungsten. He would not listen to the people who attempted to persuade him away from his fruitless efforts. He persisted. Edison's persistence gave the world electric light.

Ray Kroc of McDonald's hamburger fame hung the following quote, attributed to Calvin Coolidge, in his office:

Nothing in the world can take the place of persistence.

Talent will not. *Nothing is more common than unsuccessful people with great talent.*

Genius will not. *Unrewarded genius is almost a proverb.*

Education will not. *The world is full of educated derelicts.*

Persistence and determination alone are omnipotent.

Visionary Goal Setting

Powerful people are goal-setters with a vision. They know exactly what they want to accomplish, and they direct all their energies toward these goals. Martin Luther King Jr. had a vision of the removal of color barriers. Eleanor Roosevelt had a vision of establishing the United Nations that led to a lifetime commitment to that cause. In 1961 John Kennedy had a vision of a man on the moon "before the decade is out." We accomplished that feat in 1969, before the decade was out. It is important to know what you ultimately want — to set goals that are achievable and yet for which you have to stretch. Write them down. Set a time frame for when they will happen. Make all goals specific.

Orientation Toward the Future

Powerful people are oriented toward the future. They don't just observe the now; they analyze trends. They are alert to change, constantly searching for new challenges and options. Powerful people develop a fine sense of timing for making decisions. Their timing works because they see the trends and look to the future, and they know that today's actions will have future results. They anticipate changes in the marketplace even before these changes take place, and they're on guard for trends which will affect services.

Orientation Toward Learning and Knowledge

Powerful people have a great thirst for knowledge. They never stop learning. Successful people use every opportunity to learn through reading, listening to tapes, attending lectures, doing research and keeping an open mind.

Dave Thomas, founder of Wendy's, is a successful man by any measure. Yet he only recently got his General Educational Development or GED diploma from Coconut Creek High School in Coconut Creek, Florida. This is a powerful tribute to the fact that influential people often believe in continuous learning and improvement. Cavett Robert, another successful man and founder of the National Speakers Association, is known for saying, "School is never out for the professional."

Innovative Risk-Taking

Powerful people are risk-takers. People who are unafraid of risk project a personal power. Leaders with a strong sense of personal power know they are in charge of their lives and have responsibility for their own fate. This confidence gives them a sense of freedom, which adds to their power.

Most people who are afraid to take risks are afraid of two seeming opposites. They fear failure, and they fear success. People who fear failure are afraid of hurt, injury or a loss of some kind. If they are not willing to be wrong, however, they will never experience the exhilaration of being right. You've failed many times, although you may not remember. You fell down the first time you tried to walk. Did you hit the ball the first time you swung a bat?

R. H. Macy failed seven times before his store in New York caught on. Although its future is in doubt, no one can deny that it was a great success for many years. Babe Ruth struck out 1,330 times, but he also hit 714 home runs. Don't worry about failure. Instead, worry about the chances you miss when you fail to try.

In a study of many of the nation's top business leaders, management expert Warren Bennis found that failure was not a word in their vocabulary. These leaders thought of mistakes as learning experiences. A perfect record often means one is not taking enough risks.

One company that has long had a policy of encouraging its employees to take risks is Minnesota Mining & Manufacturing. This company allows employees to devote 15 percent of their time to projects of their own choosing. The policy is called bootlegging. One of the great bootleg successes of the 1980s was the Post-it™ Note Pads developed by researcher Art Fry. He used an adhesive that had been around for decades. The Post-it™ invention was created because Fry was frustrated at bookmarks falling out of his hymnal during church services. Post-it™ sales are now estimated at more than $300 million a year.

The other side of fear of risk is fear of success. If I succeed and make it to the next level, will I be able to handle those heavier responsibilities? Fear of success is often simply a lack of self-confidence. Stretch yourself in any way that lets you know you're exploring new territory. Suppose it is year-end and time for your performance appraisal. If all you have accomplished in your job is to maintain the status quo or hold onto existing clients, there is nothing here to call positive attention to your achievements. You have only done what is expected of you. There has been no stretching, and no growth, and this reflects a fear of success.

My first job was as Special Events Coordinator at a large department store. I was in charge of table-setting contests, celebrity visits to the stores and other special events. My work was satisfying, and I was busy striving to handle successfully all the myriad details of these various commitments.

However, I wanted to be able to point to an accomplishment that was *my* brainstorm. I took a risk. I suggested to the management that in addition to the high school fashion boards that were already in place, we also select *junior* high school fashion board members. After all, through their parents, these young eleven- to fourteen-year-old youngsters spent a great deal of money in the stores. I argued that this would differentiate our store from the other department stores in the area, that it would give the store a lot of free publicity and that it would create loyal customers: the members of the junior high school fashion boards, their parents and families.

After I convinced management to proceed, I panicked! Had I taken too great a risk? What if my suggestion failed? I need not have worried. The auditions for the sixty positions on the first junior high school fashion boards brought 1,200 young girls, their mothers and others into the store. The idea was a smash success! Even if it had failed, it was still worthwhile. The free publicity it brought to the store would have cost a fortune if we had to purchase it.

Go that step further so you can demonstrate what you personally have brought to the job that is unique, beyond the status quo. For instance, if you take every assignment and act as though you were doing it to expand your own business, you will make your employer's business more profitable. If you volunteer to do more than just what is required, your performance appraisal will reflect your actions.

Positive Attitude

Powerful people have positive attitudes, primary factors in determining success or failure in job or home life. Our attitudes are the ways we choose to think. They are our responsibility. We can choose to think negatively or positively. It is in our control.

Visualize yourself as someone who succeeds, and you will know yourself as one who succeeds. "I will" is the language of a personally powerful person. The words become a self-fulfilling prophecy.

A self-fulfilling prophecy occurs when a person's expectation of an event affects the outcome of that event. A student who believes that she is dumb will not study. The end result will be failure in school: a self-fulfilling prophecy.

"Self-talk" or mental script-writing is a process that people go through much of the time. According to many studies, as much as 77 percent of our self-talk is negative. "Why am I always so clumsy?" "What a dumb thing to do." Don't indulge in this sort of self-talk. Instead, learn the language of straight talk and position yourself more positively in your own mind.

Powerful people have a clear sense of their own self-worth, their weaknesses and strengths. Learn to turn your weaknesses into strengths. Hire people who have the skills you lack. Delegate. Take courses. One strength is knowing how to compensate for weaknesses. In that way you can stay positive and not be trapped by weakness. Here are a few ideas to help promote a positive attitude.

Speak and think positive thoughts. Tell yourself that you are a success. Repeat this thought twenty to thirty times. Make sure the statements are simple, direct, positive and in the present tense.

Avoid negative denials. Say "I am a good worker," not "I will not be lazy." Otherwise the concept of laziness will bury itself in your brain. You can overcome it, but it will take more effort.

Avoid the future tense. If you say, "I will be successful," your mind has no incentive to act now. Say, "I am successful." **Be firm and precise about what you want.** Say, "I am . . ." or "I have . . . ." Avoid qualifiers, such as "I'd like" or "I hope." Play these tapes in your head before going to sleep. One study showed that three out of four people who used this system said it had a positive effect on the way they viewed the world and the way the world saw them.

As guest speaker at a large hotel in Atlanta recently, I noticed that our waiter was doing an extraordinary job. He was there at the exact moment we needed him, and he thanked us for choosing that hotel. He was charming and competent. I called him over to compliment him. He replied, "I work hard to do a good job. After all, I am a professional."

I am a professional, and you are a professional. You are unique and in charge of your own destiny. If you don't like what is happening to you, change your attitude. You can't change others, but you can change your attitude toward others. It's not your problem when someone is rude or a bully. Think of that person as someone who bullies people because she is inwardly afraid. You might find your attitude toward that person will change.

Make positive thinking a habit. The words that you use are a reflection of your attitude. You invite failure when you say, "It won't work" or "I'm just a housewife."

The following statement has been attributed to S.I. Hayakawa. "Notice the difference between what happens when a person says to himself or herself, 'I have failed three times,' and what happens when that person says, 'I am a failure.'"

Making changes in language will improve your attitude. Instead of saying, "You're wrong!" say "I disagree." Instead of "You did it wrong!" say "This report is incorrect." Change "you" statements to "I" statements in which you express your feelings. Examples of ineffective "you" statements are "You

make me mad," "You never help," and "You always clam up."
"I" examples of these statements that are more effective are "I
am angry," "I need help with this," and "I often feel I don't
know what you think or feel such as when . . . ."

Program yourself every day with positive, affirmative statements and then extend that attitude to others. Choose to find
people interesting. Choose to find your life and your work a
challenge. Walter D. Wintle says it all:

> If you think you are beaten, you are.
> If you think you dare not, you don't.
> If you like to win, but you think you can't,
> It's almost certain you won't.

> If you think you'll lose, you're lost.
> For out of the world we find,
> Success begins with a person's will.
> It's all in the state of mind.

Positive thinking will let you do everything better than
negative thinking. A positive attitude will let you use the
qualities and abilities that you have.

Assertiveness

Powerful people are assertive. The word "assertive" has
some negative connotations. Being assertive is not a synonym
for being angry. Assertiveness is a communication skill, an
ability to communicate your point of view. Lack of assertiveness is not strictly a woman's problem. It is found on both
sides of the gender divide.

Assertiveness is awareness of your personal rights and a
willingness to actively defend those rights without infringing
on the rights of others. Assertiveness does not include hostile
or aggressive actions toward others. For example, expressions

of assertiveness should convey positive feelings, worth and kindness. Assertive actions include holding a door for someone, greeting a person, offering your seat in a bus, having the courage to share sincere emotions with someone or, whether you are a man or woman, being able to cry when the situation warrants it. In the workplace, assertiveness requires fairness to yourself or others, refusal to accept attempted dominance by ambitious co-workers and rejection of inappropriate language or assignments.

You are being assertive when you speak up for yourself during a performance review or when you observe some inequity related to your skills. A friend of mine named Dara held an administrative assistant job with a major corporation. Within the company there are a number of grade levels for secretarial work. Dara noticed that a few secretaries in the firm who also reported to multiple executive-level bosses and had similar work assignments were graded two levels higher than she was. Since she had always been praised for her competence, Dara felt that her grade level should be increased.

First she talked to the personnel department to see if her perception of the discrepancy was correct. Personnel confirmed Dara's observations. Then Dara asked for an appointment with one of the vice presidents to whom she reported. She brought information to back up her claim to the meeting. She presented her case in a factual, friendly manner. Shortly after that, Dara's position was raised two grade levels to executive secretary, and she received an appropriate salary increase. This promotion was a direct result of her assertive behavior.

If everyone were courteous and played by the rules, assertiveness would be unnecessary. But they don't — sometimes deliberately and probably more times thoughtlessly — so assertiveness is needed to restore a sense of justice.

- If someone interrupts you when you're speaking, it is assertive to say, "Tom, I would like to finish my statement."
- If someone asks you for a ride home and it's inconvenient and the drive will take you out of your way, it's assertive

to say, "I'm pressed for time today. I can take you to a convenient bus stop, but I won't be able to take you home."

There is a fine line between assertiveness, passivity and aggression. Passivity means failing to stand up for yourself so that your rights are easily violated. Sometimes people deliberately challenge you because they know you won't make waves when they use you. If you must have your way continually, must be in control and see others as a means to an end, you are more aggressive than assertive. Aggressiveness means violating other people's rights. The assertive person is tactfully honest and direct. She takes responsibility for her own feelings and avoids placing blame. He understands the other's position but communicates his own rights. Intent determines how any given behavior should be interpreted. For example, if the intent or aim is to please, the person is probably more passive than assertive.

We have looked at a number of behaviors and habits of thought that are common among personally-powerful people. Leaders have persistence. They are goal-setters, future-oriented and knowledge-oriented. Powerful people are risk-takers. They consistently have a positive attitude and use assertive behavior. These straight-talk behaviors from within are most likely to occur in people who develop healthy self-esteem, feelings of self-worth and a strong sense of confidence.

5
Self-Esteem, Confidence, Self-Worth

Without healthy self-esteem it's hard to be a success at anything. Sound self-esteem is liking yourself and feeling good about yourself. Actors must have a healthy sense of self-esteem. Without confidence there is no way an actor can learn a variety of roles, step on a stage in front of huge numbers of people and communicate with audiences. All of these actions take confidence and feeling good about oneself. This principle applies no less to the business world.

The most important decision you make every day is how you feel about yourself, that is, your self-confidence or self-esteem. A strong sense of *self* feeds positive attitudes. Your self-image affects your activities, feelings and abilities. It's not who you are but who you *think* you are that limits accomplishments.

Self-esteem has a personal meaning for me. When I was in junior high school, I was quite tall. I was my current height, 5 feet 11 inches, at age thirteen. Since I was also very thin and gangly, it took all my powers of concentration to make my arms and legs go in the right direction. I was very self-conscious about my height, since most of the boys my age were at least a foot shorter. I thought that if I slouched I could make myself look smaller and people wouldn't notice my height.

One day my Dad said to me, "If you're trying to hide your height, that won't work! Poor posture only calls attention to you. Because you are tall, when you enter a room people are going to notice you. That's a given. It seems to me that you have two choices. You can slouch, and they can feel sorry for your lack of confidence — that's choice number one. Or, choice number two, you can stand tall with excellent posture, and they will see a statuesque, regal-looking, self-assured young woman. The choice is yours. Which would you rather be?"

I took Dad's comments to heart and thought about them a lot. I started to practice good posture. It wasn't long before I realized he was right. The choice was up to me. If I had excellent posture, people would notice my height in a positive way. The more positive feedback I got, the more positive I felt about myself. And the taller I stood!

Over-confidence or false confidence can create problems. A college professor once told one of his students that there was no excuse for poor spelling. He said, "You should consult a dictionary whenever you are in doubt. It's as simple as that." The student appeared confused. "But, sir," he replied, "I'm never in doubt."

There's a fine line between feeling good about yourself, knowing you are good at something and being egocentric. Egotism is false self-esteem. How much modesty is false modesty? Maybe Mort Sahl was right when he said, "The height of egotism is humility."

We are taught as young children not to brag about ourselves. Sometimes we confuse this with "It isn't nice to think well of ourselves." That is a mistake. We need to know we are good at something, that we have a singular talent, that we are special. It isn't bragging to tell people about your skills. Each of us is a completely unique person with a combination of characteristics and experiences which makes us capable of special achievements or accomplishments. We can realistically recognize our strengths and build on them positively only when we like and respect ourselves.

Psychologist and philosopher William James is reported to have asked, "Do I run because I am frightened or am I frightened because I run?" "As a man thinketh in his heart, so is he," quotes the Book of Proverbs. And Shakespeare tells us, "There is nothing either good or bad, but thinking makes it so." There are those among us who go through life blaming spouses, children, bosses and co-workers for their miseries. They see themselves as victims of events.

It is true that we live in a negative environment of wars, earthquakes, violence, mayhem and murder. In this environment, fear is built in, and it is difficult to maintain healthy self-esteem. Our self-image affects our activities, feelings and abilities. It isn't who we are but rather who we *think* we are that limits us.

Buddha said, "What you think, you become." If you dwell on the idea that you are clumsy or homely, you give energy to that idea, you come to believe it and, when you believe something, you act on it. In a way you actually become clumsy or homely.

Poor self-esteem develops in a person in three ways: receiving negative strokes, ignoring merits and rewarding mistakes and incorrect behavior. Many people in our lives inadvertently contribute to our poor self-esteem.

Receiving Negative Strokes

Poor self-esteem begins when we are very young and our parents, older siblings or the neighborhood children don't want us to get swollen heads, so they put us in our place. Our teachers and classmates cheerfully continue that pattern. They squelch us whenever possible, for our own good.

This story of "Billy" is a composite of a series of critical life events as reported by psychologists, teachers and a key administrator in the St. Louis School System. Five-year-old Billy has already faced numerous indignities from parents and siblings. He has continually been put down the five years of his young life, and there are still more negative strokes ahead. He keeps right on being clobbered over the years by teachers, classmates and others he meets. His mother criticizes his art work to help him, and he allows this to destroy something in him and to diminish his self-esteem further. His accidents and mistakes are put on display, while his triumphs are ignored. His teachers continue the negative strokes all through school, and those strokes are counter-productive.

Ignoring Merits

When Billy gets into the working world, he encounters a similar pattern. His boss takes him for granted when he does the job right. When he asks for an evaluation, the answer is, "If I didn't like how you were doing the job, I'd have said so by now. You can assume you're doing it right unless you hear from me."

The act of paying attention is also a positive stroke. People need positive strokes; attention is like food for the emotions. If positive strokes are missing, negative ones will do. They are better than no strokes at all.

Rewarding Mistakes

Billy goes back to the job, but less enthusiastically. The manager thinks he's been supportive and has been giving feedback all day. In fact Billy still doesn't know whether he is doing well or poorly. In a few months he makes a serious mistake. His manager says, "How could you do this? Why didn't you talk to me?" Eventually Billy learns the ultimate lesson, which he passes on to a new employee: "Just stay out of trouble and earn your pay. Don't try to be a hero. We don't care for bright young apple-polishers around here." Negative attention, negative reinforcement.

If attention only comes when people make mistakes, they will make more mistakes to garner more attention, even if this is not a conscious decision. Rewards teach lessons, but not necessarily the ones we think are being taught.

How many times do we inadvertently reward children and adults for their mistakes and ignore their merits? When we do this, we stifle their creativity, enthusiasm and positive attitude and get more of the same behavior. Michael LeBoeuf's *GMP: The Greatest Management Principle* says, "The things that get rewarded, get done." Establishing the proper link between performance and reward is the greatest key to improving performance.

Many companies claim to espouse this management principle, but in practice reward behaviors they certainly don't want to promote. Here are a few questions LeBoeuf asks:

Does your company need better results but reward people who look busiest?

Does it ask for quality work but set unreasonable deadlines?

Does it ask for harmony but reward squeaking joints who complain the most?

Does it ask for teamwork but reward one team member at the expense of another?

Does it talk about frugality but award the largest budget increases to those who deplete all their resources?

These are prime examples of rewarding undesirable behavior. The result is repetition of the unwanted behavior because negative attention is better than none at all, even if it destroys self-esteem.

I know you've heard this concept before, but take a moment to think it through again. There is no one in the world like you. There is no one on the face of this earth with your fingerprints, no one with your voice prints, no one with your DNA, no one with the exact combination of your features, aptitudes and talents. You can choose to be sloppy, or you can choose to be neat. You can choose to be the most attractive, well-read person you can be, or you can give up and blame others.

When you think of yourself, what do you think? "I can't do a thing with my hair!" "I'm dumb." "They got ahead because they had all the luck!" Or do you think positive thoughts like "I know I can handle that task if I just put my mind to it."

Make a list of all the things you *can* do. Don't keep reinforcing your weak areas by repeating what they are. Instead, do something about them. For instance, if you have trouble remembering things, don't keep excusing yourself by saying, "I have a bad memory." Work every day to improve your memory. Learn helpful techniques, such as listening with concentration to the names you hear, repeating the names as soon as you hear them. Think of adjectives that begin with the same letters of the names, ones that somewhat describe the other's personalities.

But concentrate on what you are doing, or this method can backfire! An amusing incident relating to this method happened to me many years ago. A memory expert friend of mine used the adjective, patrician, to help him remember my name, Patricia. A few weeks later I received a letter from him addressed to the "Patrician *Priscilla* Ball!" Once you have achieved a few successes with this technique, you will become more confident in your ability to remember and consequently will improve your memory.

What you feed your mind becomes a self-fulfilling prophecy. If you say, "I can't lose weight," then you won't lose weight. Instead say, "I will lose weight by____," and give yourself a goal, a deadline. After Oprah failed at her first permanent weight-loss attempt, she set goals and changed her lifestyle and only then did she succeed.

Differences between the success levels of people are often related to differences in their levels of confidence, self-esteem and self-worth. Believe in yourself. Feel good about yourself and your abilities. The *choice* to do so is up to you. You make choices every day of your life. You choose to find life a series of difficult problems or exciting challenges. You choose to find people interesting or boring. You choose to be the best informed, most attractive person you can be or to give up and blame others for your failures. Take responsibility for your own actions. Become pro-active. Learn accountability. Your success level is largely up to you.

6

Powerful Behavioral Tools

Listening Skills

Nothing is more important in acting than listening to the other characters on stage. "Acting" is actually "re-acting." The metaphor can be transferred to real-life situations. The art of effective listening is the paramount skill for straight talk. Studies indicate that most people spend from 70 to 80 percent of their workday communicating with others. Listening accounts for 45 percent of *that* time. Yet, how many people use this listening time effectively?

It's important to understand the difference between "listening" and "hearing." "Hearing" is the process by which sound travels from the ears to the brain. It requires passive involvement and very little effort. "Listening" is the process of interpreting and understanding what is heard. Listening picks up where hearing leaves off. It requires active involvement.

There are four processes involved in effective listening. Misunderstandings can occur at any of the stages along the way. The stages are:

1. Hearing clearly requires that there be no physical impairment to create difficulty in receiving sounds. This could result from being hard of hearing, from hearing-aid distortion, or from noises in the room.

2. Understanding involves comprehending what has been said. There may be different levels of understanding. Most people are not psychic and don't know what is in the speaker's mind. They must depend on what was actually said. The following plaque hangs in my office and expresses this dilemma perfectly:

> *I know you believe you understand*
> *what you think I said,*
> *but I am not sure you realize*
> *that what you heard*
> *is not what I meant.*

3. Evaluating involves making judgments and forming perceptions. One person will perceive something entirely different from another, even though both people are hearing the same message. One person's perception is his or her reality, and the other person's perception is another reality.

4. Reacting is based on our perception — what we think was said — and the reaction itself can also color what was said, since it supports our evaluation. We react to what we have heard based on our experience, which is totally different from any other person's.

Most people are poor listeners for a number of reasons. Few people are formally trained to listen. While there are courses in writing, reading and speaking, there are very few, if any, courses in listening.

Listening requires effort. It's much easier just to hear, rather than listen. If you've ever watched the television program *Crossfire*, you have seen an excellent example of people hearing but not listening.

Children are inadvertently taught poor listening habits. Their adult role models consistently fail to pay attention to what adults say to one another. Adults constantly interrupt each other and seldom listen to children.

Poor listening creates problems both in one's work and one's personal life. Ineffective listening is partly to blame for the so-called generation gap between teenagers and parents. The cause of deteriorating marital relationships can often be traced to the failure of couples to listen to each other. One counselor told a troubled married couple that they should talk to each other more frequently. The wife said, "Oh, we talk to each other plenty. It's listening to each other that's the problem."

Poor listening is a major cause of misunderstandings between people. It is the basic cause for the end of many friendships. Eighty percent of people who fail in jobs reportedly do so because they can't get along with others. Failure to get along is caused partly by poor listening.

In business, poor listening is expensive. With more than one hundred million workers in America, a simple ten-dollar listening mistake by each worker would cost American business one billion dollars! No one knows how many letters must be retyped every day, how many customers go elsewhere because no one listens to complaints, how many jobs must be done over because someone didn't listen to instructions.

Here is a transcript of an actual phone conversation which powerfully illustrates the problems that can arise due to ineffective listening:

"Hi, Sam. It's Linda Thompson of Thompson Contractors . . . Pretty good, thanks. I'm going to be out of town for a few days, so I thought I'd call my trusty lawyer to check on the outcome of the attachment for the Sunrise Drive Apartment Complex . . . . The court date is set for next *Tuesday*, the 29th? What good is that going to do me? . . . I know you explained how getting the attachment was my only safe option. So maybe you can explain to me how you'll get the judge to go along with an attachment next Tuesday, when the Sunrise Drive Complex was bought by the out-of-town firm last *Thursday!* . . . Yes, last *Thursday*, on the 29th — not this month! The 29th of June, not July . . . I said June, and because you can't tell the difference between June and July, I just lost $15,000 the Sunrise Drive Apartments owed me for installing smoke detectors . . . This is going to put me right out of business, and what are you going to do about that, Mr. Big Shot Lawyer? . . . *Listen?* . . . You want me to listen? . . . You're the one who should have listened and let me tell you . . . ." And the transcript goes on.

Clearly a communication problem occurred here. But even if the lawyer had been given the wrong date, he could have saved the client from bankruptcy by knowing how to listen — by paying attention, asking questions and restating the information to ensure that it was correct.

Effective listening can bring great benefits. Everyone needs recognition. One of the easiest ways to give workers recognition is to take the time to listen to them. Furthermore, workers may point out things that can be done better and therefore more profitably, if you are willing to listen to them. The importance of being a good listener cannot be overestimated.

Listening can't be a passive activity. It is a full-time, active effort that takes into consideration words and their meanings, tone of voice, emphasis and nonverbal clues. You cannot be planning your rebuttal and still listen to what someone is saying.

Imagine what it would be like to work for an organization where telephone calls were never misdirected and the correct merchandise was always shipped because every person listened to requests and instructions. Every solicitation would result in a sale because salespeople would listen to what the customer wants. There would be no antagonism between supervisors and employees because each would understand the others' problems and needs. Impossible? Perhaps, but we can certainly strive for that sort of perfection.

We need to learn the art of effective listening. There are a number of common listening problems which interfere with the listening process.

Do personal biases encourage you to "tune out" some people? I have recorded many commercials. Early in my career I was on my way to an audition. I felt particularly good about the way I looked that day. I had on a new suit and freshly-polished shoes, and my hair looked great. I had done an excellent job of putting myself together. When I stepped onto the elevator, I found myself staring at the only other person there.

He was unkempt, with a scraggly beard and hair longer than mine that looked as if it hadn't been washed for a year. The waist of his tattered blue jeans didn't quite reach the bottom of his frayed, plaid shirt, so a number of unruly hairs peeked out from the gap between pants and shirt. He was wearing unpolished, rundown, scuffed loafers and no socks. The final touch was his eyes, beady with a lot of white showing, and I thought of them as Charles Manson eyes.

He looked at me and said, "Hi, man!" I was terrified! I made a careful study of the toes of my shoes, anxiously waiting for the elevator to stop at my destination. After what seemed like an eternity, the elevator stopped at my floor, I hurriedly got off and headed down the hallway to the audition suite. Suddenly I was aware that I was being followed. When I looked around, there was "Charles Manson" right behind me! I spotted the room where the audition was to be held, pushed open the door, slammed it shut and blockaded it with my body. "Charles Manson" pushed the door (with me against it) open and walked past me into an office directly in front. When he closed the office door, I noted a sign that read **DIRECTOR**. Although I did not get cast in the commercial that day, I learned a valuable lesson. Keep an open mind. Don't allow personal biases or prejudices to get in the way of the listening process.

Are you aware that you can think four times as fast as you can talk, which provides time for the mind to wander? Everyone has had the following experience. You are in a conversation with a female friend. She mentions her spouse in passing. Suddenly you find yourself thinking of *your* spouse, and you mentally relive an argument the two of you had that morning. Minutes later you "return to earth" and realize the other person has been speaking for some time and you have not heard a thing she has said.

Our ability to think faster than we speak is a physiological given, but there are techniques you can use to exercise your mind and capitalize on the fact that thought is faster than speech. Paraphrase, in your own words, what has been said.

Summarize. Weigh the pros and cons. Do you agree or disagree with what has been said? Listen between the lines. Is there a hidden agenda?

Do you jump to conclusions instead of listening to the entire thought? There are two methods of listening, anticipating and assuming. Anticipating is done with an open mind. You *think* you know where the conversation is going, but you listen more carefully to make sure you are correct. Another kind of anticipation occurs when you have no idea where the conversation is going, but you want to get information. Therefore, you listen more attentively. When you assume, you believe that you know where the conversation is going. Therefore, you stop listening to the other person and fabricate your own version of the conversation according to your assumptions.

My four-year-old son, David, got into some trouble, and I was chastising him. I said, "David, did you do that intentionally?" David responded almost eagerly, "Yeh, that's right! I did it intentionally!" His response further angered me. I punished him and sent him to his room. Later that evening, still smarting over his punishment, David tearfully asked his father, "Dad, what does 'intentionally' mean?" As it turned out, he thought intentionally meant accidentally.

He was punished for something that was indeed an accident. Be sure you understand all the facts before you make a judgment. Righteous indignation falls into this category. Hold your fire. Don't judge until you understand completely. Instead of imposing pre-conceived ideas on what you hear, carefully examine objective evidence. As you can see, different perceptions of word meanings can create communication misunderstandings.

Do you listen for details instead of broad ideas and concepts? The mind can only absorb so many details. If you have no idea what the broad themes of a conversation are, your mind might randomly choose to remember unimportant details and omit important ones. I'm sure you have seen a person who takes voluminous notes during a meeting, writing down every word. If you missed the meeting and asked what the most important agenda items were, the notetaker would not be able to tell you. He would have to look at the notes again to give you even the gist of what was discussed. Find areas of interest and listen for ideas first and foremost, rather than details. Make sure you understand the big picture, the larger concept.

Do you judge a person by her manner of delivery instead of what she is saying? One of my college professors sprinkled his lectures liberally with "ers" and "ums." I began counting the "ers" and "ums" and didn't hear any of the other words. I almost failed the course. A mesmerizing delivery can affect you in the same way. You find yourself lulled by the very dynamism of the speaker. I believe this is what happened to the world when Hitler or Jim Jones spoke. Judge the content of what is being said, not the delivery.

Do you give in to physical distractions? I was presenting a seminar in Florida on a bright, sunny day. We were on the third floor of a building which had glass walls. We looked out onto a sand beach, with waves crashing against the shore. Children were playing, people were sunbathing and the palm trees were swaying. Everyone in the room was looking out onto the beach — including me! I created some easy exercises to distract the audience, and we ended the seminar early. It takes effort, but work at listening and resist distractions. Distractions can be mental as well as physical.

Finally, don't think about what you're going to say while the other person is talking. When my daughter was a little girl, she made a brilliant statement that has stuck with me ever since. "What did you say, Mom? I didn't hear you. I had my own answer running!" She said that because I was chastising her. Be very careful when you are listening to someone that you are not listening with your "answer running."

A client who met Sigmund Freud once wrote, "The attention Freud gave me, the appreciation of what I said, even when I said it badly, was extraordinary. You have no idea what it meant to be listened to like that." When you listen to someone, you're not just absorbing information. You are validating that person. You are giving him or her a sense of self-worth.

One way to turn your attention to others is to escape from the "I" or "my" practice. Talk to others without using these words. Instead use "you" or "your." Ask three good open-ended questions in a row and really listen to the answer. Listening is re-acting, not acting. Use active listening, which means re-stating in your own words what the other has said, reflecting both the intellectual content and emotional feelings of what was said. Remember, paraphrasing doesn't imply agreement, just acceptance that the other person has a right to that feeling or statement. A key element to active listening is empathy or putting yourself in the other person's shoes. Listen with the speaker's point of view. Respond to the feelings expressed or to the unexpressed ones that you sense. A statement such as "I sense that you have some concerns about this" might bring a more open reaction.

Use pauses effectively. People are afraid of pauses and silences. They'll rush to fill in the space, which will provide you with more information and allow you to respond more effectively.

The first step to being a good listener is to stop talking. Saying nothing often shows a fine command of language. The Greek philosopher Zeno put it best: "We have been given two ears, but a single mouth, in order that we may hear more and speak less." Stop talking, and then ask questions.

Asking questions is a wonderful listening device. Ask questions not for the sake of having something to say, but out of a desire to understand. The question you ask may not be as important as the way in which you ask it. A young monk observed an older monk smoking a pipe while praying. The young monk waited until the older one finished praying, then approached him and said, "Are you sure you should be smoking while you are praying? When I entered the monastery I asked the father if it would all right if I smoked while I pray and he answered, "Absolutely not, my son. I'm surprised that you even asked."

The older monk turned to the younger and said, "Your problem is that you didn't ask the right question. Years ago I asked the father the same question but in a slightly different way. I asked, "Father, is it all right if I pray while I smoke?" He answered, "Of course, my son! That's an excellent idea!"

Skillful questions are tools we can use to break down barriers. Don't ask, "May I help you?" That is a closed-ended question, one where it is easy to get a no answer. Closed-ended questions are often answered with one word, usually a yes or a no, and serve to end the communication process. Open-ended questions require a longer and more complex answer, which in turn provides additional information. Instead of the closed-ended question above, "May I help you?" ask "How may I be of service?" You might get some information with this question that will help close a sale, solve a problem or help you to persuade someone. Another good leading question is, "Tell me a little bit about what you are looking for." Then stop talking and listen to the response. The customer might reveal his or her interest and buying style by the answer.

Asking questions skillfully will:

1. Raise the customer's response level, that is, get the customer to talk. Say something like "Why do you say that?"

2. Provide an opportunity for the customer to get involved in the selling situation. Ask a question, such as "Which color would you prefer?"

3. Ask for information needed to close the sale, such as "Tell me something about your lifestyle, so I can recommend the right one for your needs."

4. Create trust by asking about examples: "Would you be interested in looking at one of the jobs we have completed for a satisfied client?"

5. Discover erroneous information the customer has about your company or product and respond, "That information is no

longer valid. That was the case a few years ago, but that problem has been corrected for some time now."

Telephone Talk

Talking on the telephone requires special listening techniques. When speaking on the phone, let the other person do half the talking. After all, most face-to-face conversations between two people consist of each one speaking half the time. If the person to whom you are speaking gets the impression you are not listening, she will stop listening too.

Remember to ask open-ended questions on the phone. Instead of asking, "Did you receive the material I sent?" ask, "What did you think of the material I sent?" You'll get more information.

Pay attention to what the person on the other end is saying. Avoid thinking about what you are going to say next while the other person is speaking.

Encourage the person to keep talking by making it obvious that you are listening. Don't let long periods go by without saying anything. Inject comments about what the other person is saying whenever appropriate. Let the other person know you understand. Ask questions about what she is saying. Show that you're interested in her point of view.

In summary, work at listening! By listening effectively you learn about others, their ideas and needs and the best way to reach them. You give them a sense of self-worth. You make them respect and listen to you. Aren't those benefits worth the effort?

Charles Eliot, former president of Harvard, is reputed to have said, "There is no mystery about successful business interaction. Exclusive attention to the person who is speaking to you is important. Nothing else is so flattering as that."

Gender Communication Skills

Understanding the ways in which women and men have traditionally been taught to communicate helps an actor arrive at a solid conception of the character she will play. Understanding those same patterns will help everyone to respect and effectively deal with communication in everyday life. By the year 2000 nearly half of the workers in America will be women. It only makes sense to learn the differing communication styles of men and women, because each of us will know how to communicate effectively with the other half of the work force.

Research shows that there are many differences between male and female communication styles; being aware of these differences is often beneficial. The ideal style of communication blends the best aspects of both styles. When we learn to understand and respect the communication differences between men and women, we can make those differences work for us. Clashes between the sexes can be reduced and even eliminated if each gender works to understand the other's communication techniques. There is no reason for women to adopt men's style or vice versa. What is necessary is recognition and respect for the other style. The ideal in the workplace incorporates both female and male values and styles.

According to Alice Sargent, author of *The Androgynous Manager:**

> Men and women should learn from one another without abandoning successful traits they already possess. Men can learn to be more collaborative and intuitive, yet remain result-oriented. Women need not give up being nurturing in order to learn to be comfortable with power and conflict.

*Reprinted, with permission of the publisher, from *The Androgynous Manager* by Alice G. Sargent, 1983, AMACOM, a Division of the American Management Association. All rights reserved.

Behavioral Differences

When we discuss gender or cultural differences of any kind, we must understand that there are exceptions to every statement we make. When we lump all of one sex into a behavior category, we are stereotyping. Stereotypes are thoughts, attitudes and beliefs so strongly held that they may become self-fulfilling prophecies — we see what we expect to see. Stereotyping is reflected by statements regarding a group of people, lumping the entire group together. Our view is so firmly entrenched that there can be no open, honest communication. All of us hold stereotypes; that is not the problem. Using them to make unfavorable comparisons and to prejudge individual abilities is the problem. Unfortunately, stereotyping of male and female roles is continually reinforced in advertising, in the classroom, on television and at home.

The fact that stereotypes exist and can be misused does not mean that patterns of behavior do not exist. Being aware of the cultural differences and the socialization processes that created these differences helps us understand each other better. Once the cultural differences have been examined, it is necessary to examine the individual and whether or not she fits that cultural pattern.

Differences in Methods for Building Relationships

There are many areas of communication which reflect gender differences. One of the most noticeable concerns men's and women's attitudes toward building relationships. Men generally focus on the end result — getting the job done — and are not as interested in minute details along the way. Women are also concerned with the end result, but they pay more attention to the details and to the people with whom they interact.

In training sessions, I have observed that when men enter the room they will frequently be single focused, looking straight ahead. They mark their territory by putting a briefcase, notebook or some such item on the table and only then notice the other people in the room. "Oh, hi, Charley! I didn't see you when I came in." Whether this is an example of male result-orientation or male dominance games, as someone has suggested, the result is the same: people come second. Many women, on the other hand, pause just inside the door to the training room, stand for a moment and look around to see who is there. For them, finding a seat is less important than relationships with people.

Building relationships is a goal in itself for women. Men see relationships as a way to get things done. You can see the difference between male and female approaches if you watch children play. When the girls disagree, they must resolve their differences immediately. Relationships have to become harmonious before they can go back to playing together. It is easier for boys to play with other boys they don't like. Their play is more likely to be game- or sports-oriented, and their games have rules for resolving differences and conflicts fairly and impersonally. In baseball, football, soccer and other sports, rules for winning and losing are clear-cut. In playing house, once considered a girl's game, a judgment call has to be made as to who is the mommy and who is the child. There are no prescribed rules. As girls cross over into areas traditionally considered boys' play and vice versa, it will be interesting to see how these changes impact their adult behavior.

Differences in Major Goals for Men and Women

In her book, *You Just Don't Understand*, Dr. Deborah Tannen contends that another goal of men is independence. As children, boys are rewarded by parents, teachers and others for being self-reliant. Girls, on the other hand, are protected from real or imaginary threats.

Women's major goal is intimacy. Again, this harks back to a basic childhood-play mode. Little girls spend hours telling their innermost secrets to a best friend. If a woman wants commitment but a man is committed to freedom, you can see how these different goals would create conflicts.

Suppose a husband and wife are having a discussion. The wife says, "A terrible thing happened to me today!" and then proceeds to tell her mate about the distressing incident. The husband listens briefly and then interrupts her, offering a solution to the problem. She is suddenly exasperated. All she wanted from him was for him to listen to the whole story, offering an occasional "That must have felt awful" or "What happened next?" Because his unconscious goal is independence, he needs to be a problem-solver. She needs for him to understand how the incident made her feel. She wants empathy, not solutions. After this conversation, both husband and wife may feel frustrated and misunderstood.

This dynamic of inter-gender communications also helps explain why most men are hesitant to ask for directions. Asking directions makes them momentarily dependent on another for a solution to a problem, and they prefer to drive out of their way rather than be beholden to someone else.

Shortly after I married my husband we decided to go to dinner at a restaurant where I had eaten long before. I thought I remembered how to get there. When we came to a cross street where I believed the restaurant was located, my husband pulled up to the stop sign, looked at me confidently and said, "Which way?" I asked him to pull farther into the intersection, thinking I could recognize something familiar by looking down each side. I finally admitted that I didn't have a clue where the restaurant might be. He was upset but undaunted. He decided to find the place using only his own sense of direction. We spent an hour searching. Finally I said, "Why don't you stop at a filling station and ask directions? Admit it, we're lost!" Furiously, he said, "We are not lost! I just don't know where we are, that's all!"

Differences in Socialization Processes

Another behavioral difference is that men and women are socialized in totally different ways. Men are socialized to believe that power and ability are most important to control their environment. Women are socialized to believe that relationships are the most important means to achieve such control. One obvious example is the way men strive for power and dominance in conversations at work. They engage in competitive turn-taking by interrupting each other.

Women, on the other hand, were traditionally trained to be little ladies and told it was rude to interrupt. They were brought up to be manners teachers. This process of socialization explains why, in a heated discussion in a conference room, men will interrupt each other frequently, while a woman is more likely to wait patiently for a break in the conversation — a break which never comes. When the meeting is over, the men might assume incorrectly that she was quiet because she had nothing to say.

Advice for women: When interrupted, assert yourself. Don't let people interrupt you. There are many approaches to take. You can just continue talking. You can keep score in a good-natured way. "That's three times you've interrupted me, John. My turn now?" The best approach is as follows: use the nonverbal gesture of arm extended in front of you, with palm facing the other person in a stop signal. Use the other person's name. Then use an "I need" statement: "John, I need to finish my thought." Also, don't be the first to withdraw from an argumentative situation. Don't be intimidated by males who speak forcefully.

Advice for men: When you catch yourself interrupting others: STOP. Instead, use your listening skills. Nothing is as flattering or powerful as careful attention to what another person has to say. Concentrate on understanding the other's point. When you do speak, react to the conversation. Support others who are being interrupted by saying, "I believe Ted wants to make a point. Let's listen to what he has to say."

Differences in the Handling of Emotions

Another behavioral difference between men and women has to do with the way each gender handles aggression, anger and emotions in general. Our culture has rules about which emotions men and women should show and how they should express them. The most common, traditional messages which we receive about feelings are summarized in the diagram.

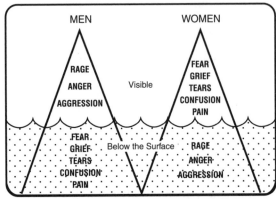

MEN   WOMEN

RAGE
ANGER   Visible   FEAR
AGGRESSION   GRIEF
TEARS
CONFUSION
PAIN

FEAR   Below the Surface   RAGE
GRIEF   ANGER
TEARS   AGGRESSION
CONFUSION
PAIN

ICEBERG OF EMOTIONS

Above the surface, the visible parts of the iceberg represent the emotions each gender is allowed by society to express in public. One iceberg represents men, the other represents women.

Men are allowed to express, though not act out, anger, aggression and rage. Women can show confusion, tenderness, grief and fear. Below the surfaces of both icebergs are the emotions men and women cannot express openly, the "male" emotions for women and the "female" emotions for men. Traditionally men and women are almost exactly the opposite in what they show and what they hide because they've been given opposite messages about what is permitted and what is forbidden.

Therefore, both sexes often display masked emotions, as opposed to what they are actually feeling inside. Aggressive, angry-looking behavior may conceal feelings of sadness, confusion, fear, pain and even affection. Many women, on the other hand, hide anger with crying, smiling or looking confused. Never assume that what you see is a clear barometer of the subject's feelings.

For men, in dealing with women: Women's tears in the workplace are rarely about sadness and loss. Sometimes a woman will break into tears and walk away from a situation when she is angry. When you see a woman looking tearful, do not move in to calm, touch or take care of her. Do not try to fix the situation. Stay where you are and ask her what she wants to say or do. Make a leading statement or ask a leading question, "If I were in your situation, I would be upset too" or "What exactly happened?"

For women, in dealing with men: Men's anger can mean a lot of different things. A man may yell, "What the hell is going on here?" when he is uncertain, confused or even fearful. When a man looks or sounds angry, do not walk away unless you are in physical danger. Instead, encourage him to talk more. Ask about what is going on and what he believes is taking place. Try to read between the lines. Get him to face and express the masked emotion that he may be unconsciously feeling.

Showing emotions, even crying in the workplace, can indicate a deep commitment to the job. However, since crying is inappropriate in a work setting, here are some pointers for women to consider when on the verge of crying:

- When it comes to crying, DON'T.
- If there is time, excuse yourself and deal with the situation at another time when you are more in control.
- Determine the actual emotion you are feeling and express it clearly.
- Continue talking. It is difficult to cry and talk at the same time.

Differing Management Styles of Men and Women

According to a study reported in the September 7, 1985, *Wall Street Journal*, women managers have different styles from male managers. Female managers tend to focus primarily on the task to be done and to work closely with employees. Women managers interact more with their workers than do male managers. This close attention often means a hands-on approach that some male employees resent. They think the attention means that the boss lacks confidence in them. Male managers focus more on themselves and their authority, delegate heavily and involve themselves less in their workers and day-to-day business matters.

Advice for men: Learn to work more closely with employees. Male managers should strengthen their interpersonal skills.

Advice for women: Learn to delegate more. The Wonder Woman syndrome is so ingrained in women that there is often a need to prove one's abilities by trying to do it all.

Differences in the Establishment of Trust

Another difference is how men and women establish trust. Women establish trust by talking and self-disclosure. When we were little girls, we played with our best friend and we told her all of our secrets. We would confide our frailties, our uncertainties and our inabilities. Our goal was to have the friend understand how and why we felt a certain way. This self-disclosure often put our feelings on the line and made us vulnerable to hurt. This is one reason why women are often sabotaged by other women in the workplace. When a woman confuses friendliness with friendship at work and carries this childhood pattern of telling all to co-workers, she occasionally finds that the self-disclosure is used against her.

Men establish trust on the basis of track records. They prove their worth to their friends by sticking with them through hardships, by bonding and by supporting each other. However, they seldom confide their innermost secrets to their friends. Self-disclosure is often considered a sign of weakness by men. In military terms it amounts to giving information to the enemy. Little boys spend more time doing than talking. They play many group games. They learn independence and organizational skills from games.

One word of advice: Be careful about disclosing too much too soon in the workplace. Don't confuse friendliness with friendship. People often make friends in the workplace and assume their new friends can be trusted. This trust is often misplaced. If you don't know your friends well enough, they may eventually sabotage you.

Differences in Team Spirit/Attitude

Team spirit and team attitude are behavioral differences between men and women that are narrowing as today's career women become more savvy. Men have traditionally been better team players, but the fact that young girls play team sports and many adult women like and understand team sports has carried into the workplace. Many people believe that men are better team players, so the differences still exist.

According to a study done by Lu Heck and Associates, a New York outplacement firm, women are sometimes let go for such classic reasons as inability to delegate or not being a team player. Team spirit and team attitude may not come easily to many women, yet they form an intrinsic part of the business world. A team member has a definite assigned position to play. Everyone needs to pay attention to what his or her team position is on the job and what duties are associated with that position. Doing one's job on the team and not getting into an area that is another person's duty is an important rule to remember.

When you think about it, the fundamentals of management skills are the same as the fundamentals of football: perceiving the goal, figuring how to reach it, motivating the team to do it and being prepared to counteract attempts to prevent it. Men love sports, understand sports, feel comfortable with sports. With the team concept being such an integral part of the business world, it helps men bond together in a familiar male camaraderie. Women, even today, do not have a similar set of experiences to draw upon.

Verbal/Language Differences

Men and women use language in different ways. Women often make indirect statements, and men often make direct statements. A woman is more likely to say, "Don't you think it would be better . . . ?" A man would probably say, "I believe it would be better . . . ." Unfortunately for the woman, direct speech is the accepted norm for the business world. People forget the woman's indirect idea and credit the man with the suggestion.

This unequal dynamic inherent in male and female communication styles was brought home to me forcefully many years ago. During my first year on the Board of Directors of the National Speakers Association, I proposed an excellent idea. At that time the board of nineteen members included only two women. In my eagerness to make my point, I forgot to frame my suggestion in direct as opposed to indirect terms. I said, "I was wondering what you thought about the idea of . . . ?" The board batted the idea around the table for a few minutes. Then a male board member said, "I move that we . . ." and proposed *my* idea! That proposal will forever be remembered as his idea. To this day, I believe he got credit because I used indirect instead of direct speech to propose my idea.

Another more subtle example of indirectness has to do with the way in which women send metamessages. A metamessage is a communication that has a hidden meaning. It can be verbal, nonverbal or a combination of both. Men send metamessages as well, but women are masters at this skill. A metamessage can communicate volumes. Have you known of a woman who spotted her spouse across a crowded room and gave him a look which said, "Let's get out of here!" He usually understands immediately and makes hasty excuses to the host. My husband chuckles at me when I say, looking and sounding utterly exhausted at six-thirty in the evening after a hard day's work, "What would you like for dinner?" This is said from a "couch potato" position. He has learned over many years of marriage that if the table is not set for dinner this means "Let's eat out!"

Some examples of nonverbal metamessages are a raised eyebrow, a frown and a long look at one's watch. Each can signal a very specific meaning to a person who knows and understands the person sending the metamessage.

When she uses metamessages, a woman expects her significant other to feel or think the same way she does and to be able to read her mind.

Some years ago my husband and I were driving to Florida. I needed to use the ladies' room and noticed that we were approaching an exit. I said to my husband, "Are you hungry?" He said, "No," and continued driving past the exit. I sat there fuming for another few miles. About a half-hour later I asked again if he was hungry. Again he said, "No," and we passed up another exit. I wanted him intrinsically to know what I was thinking and what I needed, so I sent a metamessage. When I finally realized what I had been doing, I said, "I need to use the ladies' room, really soon, in a bad way. Let's get off at the next exit." He said, "Fine. Why didn't you say so earlier?"

Common Military/Sports Metaphors

Men use a great many sports and military metaphors in business. Typical sports metaphors are the following:

• We've got to keep our eye on the ball.

- The ball's in your court.
- I like to think that I'm the quarterback.
- Someone's got to run interference.
- Joe's really out in left field.
- What we don't need is Monday-morning quarterbacking.
- A good manager's like a playing coach.
- At times a good manager must be a blocking back.
- He's batting about .333 on his decisions.
- When in doubt, punt.
- It's time for a full court press.

Military jargon includes:

- You be our point man. He is the person who walks first in a patrol, the first to be shot in an ambush and the one who has to break trail in rough country.
- An attack is a move to gain sales.
- A battle is a confrontation with a competitor.
- To bite the bullet is to face a painful fact.
- To keep your head down is to stay out of the line of fire.
- Strategy is part of the long-range plan.

Women are less likely than male employees to understand this terminology. Suppose a male manager says to a male employee, "I like to think I'm the quarterback." He communicates a number of messages. "Watch out. I've heard you, but I've already made up my mind. You're treading on shaky ground. You're forgetting who's boss."

The male employee will laugh good naturedly and say, "It was worth a try." No feelings were hurt. They spoke each other's language. But suppose it were a female employee? She might well say, "So?" She might keep arguing her point. Then she might be branded as having an uncooperative team attitude, all because she didn't know the nuances of quarterback. If a man were told, "Your job is to run interference," he would know that his job entailed clearing a path and easing the workload of an important player: the ball carrier. His job would be to complete assignments that speed the ball carrier on his way, not carry the ball himself.

Most women have never been in the army, yet collecting a salary from a business organization often means you are part of a classic military operation. The military and business world have an organized structure in common: a hierarchical command, a ranking system rating from high status to low status. The CEO and chairperson are equal to five-star generals, president is equal to general and on down. It's important to learn the appropriate chain of command and not overstep or sidestep your immediate superior.

Be aware of the close similarity between a business structure and a military operation. Take care to explain words which might be unfamiliar to your hearer. Pay attention to the different ways in which women and men think and the dissimilar words they use. Look for new metaphors that both genders understand.

Differences in How Much and How Often Men and Women Speak

What about the differences in how much and how often men and women speak? One of the myths that studies have totally exploded is that women talk too much. Many studies have shown that men speak more often and at greater length than women. The result is that women often withdraw from conversations with or involving men.

Women are more often interrupted than men. In one often-quoted study of mixed groups, men made 96 percent of all interruptions, though in single sex groups both men and women interrupt each other equally. The 96 percent figure is quoted once again by George F. Simmons and G. Deborah Weissman in *Men and Women: Partners at Work*. Dr. Deborah Tannen in *You Just Don't Understand* suggests that one of the most widely-cited findings to emerge from research on gender and language is that men interrupt women. In one sense, this is a form of unconscious competition.

Other interesting statistics in the Pamela Fishman studies relate to the introduction of topics to be discussed. According to these studies, women introduce topics 62 percent of the time. A woman might say to a man, "I read a fascinating new book recently." However, Ms. Fishman's studies find that only 36 percent of the topics that women introduce are actually discussed. Men often control the topics of conversation by switching the topic to one of interest to them. Using the above example, a man might counter by saying, "Yes, I read a new book recently too. It was about . . . ." You can see how misunderstandings can result.

Women bring up more topics in a mixed discussion. However, they are constantly interrupted by men who take over with their own contributions two-thirds of the time. Because the topic the woman brought up has been dismissed, she will frequently bow to the man's topic choice. Since that topic choice is often work or sports, women sometimes see men as being fixated on these subjects. For their part, men see women as flighty or lacking in focus, mainly because women have difficulty presenting their ideas fully. For men, this leads to the logical conclusion that women contribute less and the men fail to benefit from the women's presence on the team.

Women need to reduce their use of speech patterns that make them sound insecure. According to Robin Lakoff in *Language and Woman's Place*, women use a great deal of self-effacing language. Again, this is not suggesting that men are never guilty of using these phrases, merely that more women than men indulge in these traits.

Women use more qualifying or hedging statements than men. Words like "just," "really," "sort of" and "kind of" weaken speech. Another example of a power-robbing speech habit is the "tag" question — "We've been here a long time, haven't we?" "It's very warm in here, isn't it?" Rising inflections at the end of a sentence as in "My name is Mary Smith?" sounds as if you're asking permission. It denotes a lack of confidence and seems to ask the question, "Am I okay?" Finally, many women use the "and" syndrome, the habit of inserting the word "and" between all sentences. Perhaps women do this more than men to keep from being interrupted by men. Good traits of women's speech are that women use more words, more interesting words, and better combinations of words than men. Women have more vocal variety and express understanding and empathy better than men. Men use the speech of business better. They are more direct, factual, assertive and authoritative. However, because they don't use as many tones and inflections, men have to be careful not to use a too monotonous and boring speech pattern.

Nonverbal Gender Differences

In *Body Politics*, Nancy Henley's studies found women more sensitive to nonverbal clues than men. Perhaps this is due to the fact that women are traditionally the caretakers of children. In order to tend to the needs of very little ones, women have to understand nonverbal clues. Likewise, women are better at understanding and using tones in speech and at perceiving implications from dialogues. Perhaps this is one of the reasons that women, according to studies, are better listeners than men.

Because dominance has been the traditional role of men in business and families, we find females yielding space to males and using subordinate-to-superior nonverbal behavior with males. Women often stake out smaller personal spaces than men. Space is often related to status. The more space used, the higher the status. Men are more likely to hang an arm over an empty chair or sprawl in a chair. Women also use more closed body language. Females are conditioned from childhood to be little ladies. They are taught that it is unlady-like to stand with feet apart. Yet, from a straight talking point of view, standing with your feet firmly planted on the floor, approximately a foot apart, carries more power. You are nonverbally saying, "I can stand on my own two feet."

Inappropriate smiling behavior is also common among women. This sometimes leads to women not being taken seriously. Businessmen laugh plenty after hours and at parties, but they put much of this aside between nine and five o'clock. They learn to wipe the smile away quickly and get back to business.

With regard to expression, women's faces are much more expressive than men's. Men learn as little boys to halt tears and expressions that reveal their emotions. They are taught that displays of emotion are signs of weakness unacceptable in men.

Tilting one's head to the side is often read nonverbally as a flirtatious signal or even as submission or stupidity. Women do this routinely, especially when meeting an outstandingly dominant male. Men almost never tilt their heads to the side. Women do this for positive reasons, for example, to listen harder by turning the ear toward the speaker or to look at the person speaking. If the person speaking is taller, it may be necessary to tilt the head. In general, women tend to focus on a speaker, whether male or female, more steadily than men do. The result is that men often perceive women as uncritical listeners or even as flirts; women sometimes feel that men are arrogant.

Women tend to be touched more than men. When the touch is unwanted, it is often a status indicator — not a sexual advance. Yet what happens when women touch men, if they are not supposed to? While a man's touch is sometimes a status indicator and not necessarily sexual in nature, a woman's touch to a man is almost always interpreted sexually. In today's work climate where sexual harassment is a concern for companies, touching of any kind is risky. The only safe places for opposite genders to touch at work are between the elbow and wrist and in a handshake. Even then it is best not to shake hands for too long.

Humor as a Power Tool

Comedies are usually more popular than dramas. Humor is powerful. People love to laugh. Using humor shows that you are comfortable and that you want to make others comfortable. Using humor puts you in control. It is a particularly effective way to respond when you are verbally attacked. Humor can be a powerful tool for defusing tension.

A well-known candidate running for election years ago was asked to deliver a political speech in opposition territory. In fact, he was so disliked in that part of the country that his speaker's platform was placed over horse manure. One of the first comments out of the candidate's mouth was his thanks to the opposition for allowing him to speak from their platform!

We have had many presidents who possessed a great sense of humor. Three who immediately come to mind are Lincoln, Kennedy and Reagan.

During Abe Lincoln's presidential years, an old friend asked him how he liked being president. In response, President Lincoln said that reminded him of a story about a man who had been tarred, feathered and ridden out of town on a rail. Asked how he liked it, the man said, "Well, if it wasn't for all the attention I'm getting, I'd much rather have walked."

John Fitzgerald Kennedy was well known for his sense of humor. In the 1960 elections he was accused of using his family's wealth to unfair advantage. On hearing the accusation, Kennedy told reporters that he wanted to read a telegram from his father. He read, "Dear Jack, Don't buy one more vote than necessary. I'll be damned if I'll pay for a landslide." He is also credited with saying, "Washington, D.C., is a city with all the charm of the North and all the bustling energy of the South."

As President of the United States, Ronald Reagan used humor effectively. In fact, his sense of humor helped him to get re-elected to that office! When Reagan was running for re-election, he debated his Democratic opponent Walter Mondale several times. The Mondale camp was basing much of its campaign on the claim that Ronald Reagan was too old to be president. Reagan was prepared for this. As soon as Mondale mentioned the age issue in the televised debate, Reagan stood behind the lectern and said, "I refuse to let age be an issue in this campaign. I'm not going to exploit the fact that my opponent is young and inexperienced." The whole nation laughed, and the topic of age was never mentioned again. With one sentence he defused a potentially disastrous situation.

Even President Bush — who was not known for his wit — made fun of himself in his State of the Union message. He acknowledged that his approval rating was lower then than his wife Barbara's and suggested that she sit in for him in an upcoming meeting with the Japanese.

Ann Richards, ex-governor of Texas, spoke at a National Democratic Convention a number of years ago. She said, "George Bush was born with a silver foot in his mouth." She received a standing ovation from the Democratic crowd and was immediately catapulted from a relatively unknown politician into the national limelight.

In a series of studies, 98 percent of CEOs overwhelmingly stated a preference for job candidates with a sense of humor. Yet, when asked to name qualities that kept women from succeeding, lack of humor was at the top of the executives' list. Since it seems that women have more difficulty with humor than men, the following examples depict use of humor in the workplace by women. Obviously, both men and women can benefit from the use of humor.

Demonstrate your confidence by using humor to persuade. A woman sales representative failed repeatedly to get a meeting with a company president. When she asked him to lunch, he said that he didn't take time for lunch. Still she persisted, "Okay, I'll bring the bread, cheese and ants, and we'll have a picnic at your desk." He laughed and set up an appointment for the following week.

A woman can defuse a sexist remark by using humor. A female executive, age forty, spent a three-hour meeting with a male colleague and a male client. Over and over again, the male client referred to her as "young lady." Her male colleague grew increasingly uncomfortable and audibly whispered to her, "Are you going to let him get away with that?" "Why not?" she responded in an equally loud tone of voice. "At my age, it's a compliment."

You can convey authority through humor. When you are challenged, you can confirm your authority by making light of the *situation* without humiliating the challenger. A woman executive was presiding over a meeting. A late-arriving man commented, "I only came to this meeting because you are so pretty." She replied, "Then you should be <u>pretty</u> interested in what I have to say." Instead of making a defensive or angry retort, she made it clear that she was in charge and that she was not going to let his comment undermine her authority.

Humor defuses conflict. A woman accountant had the ticklish problem of bringing up a ten-month overdue bill to a valued client. She said, "Tom, you're an important client to our firm, but your bill is long overdue. We've carried you longer than your mother did!" The client laughed and wrote out a check on the spot for the overdue amount.

Learn to take risks with humor. Many times a humorous remark will cross a person's mind, but she hesitates to voice it for fear of bombing. My friend, Patricia Fripp, is an excellent speaker who is approximately five-feet tall. I am five-foot, eleven-inches tall. The only similarity between us is our first name! At a Board of Directors' dinner a few years ago, I was to receive a gift. The person presenting the gift to me introduced me as "Patricia Fripp." I thought, "I can understand the mistake. After all, we look so much alike!" The attendees there that evening also knew Patricia. They would have immediately picked up on the comment and chuckled. I hesitated a moment too long and the moment passed. I could have softened the impact of the goof, but I didn't take advantage of the opportunity. Don't hesitate. Take that risk!

Maintain a sense of humor. Learn to notice the funny situations that happen to you every day. Keep a humor notebook. Record jokes, half-baked ideas and funny phrases. Include humor in your letters, memos, minutes and reports.

I send out an extensive, six-page pre-program questionnaire to clients so that I can customize my programs for their organizations. The last question on the questionnaire is, "Have you ever had to answer this many questions before? If so, when?" Clients have fun in turn by answering in a silly way, and we begin our working relationship with a congenial meeting-of-minds.

Brighten your office with humorous posters. Put a humor bulletin board in a high-traffic area and invite people to post funny articles, cartoons, pictures and jokes.

Plan a stress-buster event on days when the going gets rough. What about an April Fool's Day on June 29 or National Left-Handers' Day? Be creative!

As you can see, being a powerful straight talker requires the mastery of a wide range of important behavioral skills. Effective communication begins with excellent listening ability. It includes understanding and respecting the opposite gender and their communication styles. It entails maintaining a thorough appreciation of the lighter side of life.

Not only is the development of behavioral skills important for the straight talker, but learning to use language powerfully can be a great asset. Making the right word choices will help you to become more persuasive and convincing.

7
Powerful Verbal Tools

During a working rehearsal, actors improve and perfect their vocal and movement skills. We need to do the same. In this chapter we'll concentrate on our vocal skills. Does your choice of words communicate power and confidence? Word choices are one way that you can persuade others. Here are some suggestions that will make your speech more authoritative.

Direct Speech

Use direct statements that include factual information. Indirect statements lack authority. They make you sound unsure of yourself. Here's an example of one such powerless phrase: "Don't you think it would be better if we assigned that account to Tom?" See how much stronger this statement is: "It would be better if we assigned that account to Tom," or "I suggest we assign that account to Tom" or "Tom gets it."

Ask direct questions. In a recent seminar someone raised a hand, and I called on her. She said, "May I ask a question?" I almost answered, "No." The fact that I responded to her hand in the air meant that permission was granted to ask a question.

Be precise. The question, "How many cartons are to be shipped?" is precise and direct. Answers should be precise too. To say "about six cartons" is hedging. Make it a straight "six cartons."

Brevity of Speech

Use few words and make your words matter. Say what you believe. Say it from your heart. Pick your words carefully and use them to paint pictures. Here are three powerful phrases that illustrate this technique: "Get into the game and stay in it." Eleanor Roosevelt; "The buck stops here." Harry Truman; and "I have a dream . . . ." Martin Luther King Jr. Powerful people, powerful phrases.

Work hard to evoke emotional images. Don't settle for the first words that come to mind. Look at these examples.

"We have nothing to give but blood, sweat, toil and tears," said Winston Churchill when he wanted to galvanize his country during World War II. He could have said, "We are going to fight hard."

"Ask not what your country can do for you, but what you can do for your country," said President John F. Kennedy when he wanted to rouse Americans to be patriotic. He didn't say, "It is important to be civic-minded."

Words that have been proven to put money in the pockets of salespeople are:
- "you," which brings the buyer into the conversation
- "profit," the reason the customer is in business
- "value," having to do with getting your money's worth
- "opinion," appealing to one's ego.

Take-charge words are also excellent such as:
- "follow me"
- "sign here"

Skilled persuaders don't ask "if." Instead, they ask "which."

Here are some power expressions that are particularly useful when creating a team spirit:
- I'm proud of you.
- Thank you!
- I understand.
- Will you help me?
- What do you think?

Here are some ways to speak more authoritatively:

A. Eliminate waffle words from your vocabulary. For example, what does "at this point in time" mean? The word "now" is more effective. Other waffle words and phrases are, "What I'm trying to say is," "in other words" or "I just wanted to say." Say it or use the other words. Think of Eliza Doolittle in *My Fair Lady.* Although the direct communications she wanted from her suitor, Freddy, were of a nonverbal nature, Eliza definitely did *not* want waffle words and flowery phrases. If you know what you want to say, be direct and brief. Using unnecessary words shows a vague grasp of your subject.

B. Weasel words weaken your speech by allowing exceptions. Advertisers use them liberally for legal protection. "Probably," "most," "usually," "generally" and "about" are a few which allow you to "weasel out" of an apparent firm statement.

C. According to a study by Yale University, the twelve most persuasive words in the English language are **free, safe, guarantee, health, save, discover, money, easy, proven, new, results** and **love.** When you are working to persuade someone, sprinkle these words throughout your message. Whenever you write anything that's designed to sell or persuade, find a way to insert some of these words.

D. Take responsibility for yourself whether the situation is a positive or a negative one. Use the "I" pronoun. For example, the statement, "We came up with this plan," does not indicate that you are the leader. A better choice would be "I formulated the idea and Jones worked out the details."

E. Express yourself in "I need" statements. For instance, instead of "Will you repeat that, I can't hear you," say, "I need for you to speak louder, I can't hear."

Cerebral Speech

Tell people what you think, not what you feel. Particularly at work, avoid emotion-laden, gut-reaction words. "I think," "I know," "I believe" and "I suggest" are much more authoritative than "I really feel" or "I just love." There are some exceptions to this rule, of course, depending on the reason for your talk. If you are in sales and speaking to a client about benefits, "you" is the most important word. In a sales situation, you want to get the client thinking with you in the direction of the sale now. You also want to encourage the client to consider the value-add-on to the sale. Finally, you hope to develop a long-range and continuous sales relationship. The pronoun "we" can be a useful tool for involving a group of people in your project. The correct authority — as opposed to authoritarian — statements should elicit a desire to follow willingly and persistently.

When responding to criticism, ask for facts to support the critic's assertions and then paraphrase the criticism. Say, "Let me make sure I understand what you're saying," and then restate the criticism using your own words. Another powerful way to deal with criticism is simply to admit your mistake. In this case, be sure to remedy the situation. *Mea culpas* without action may work in politics, but they don't fly in business. Alternatively, if you disagree with criticism, state your case without becoming emotionally involved. "I disagree. I understand why you might think that, but here is why I think differently . . . ."

Silence

Silence is powerful. Say what you need to say, and then stop talking. Most people are afraid of silence. They rush in to fill the space. Take advantage of this opportunity to listen more closely. In their eagerness to fill conversational gaps, other people may reveal weaknesses, providing you with an upper hand in adversarial situations, or give you key information to close a sale.

Learning when to be silent is particularly important in negotiations. Negotiating is a form of selling. I have something to sell, and you are here as someone who could buy. Negotiating strength comes from knowing more about the other side or person. You learn more about the other side when you are quiet and listen, allowing them to talk. In negotiations it is often said that the first person to speak, loses.

Speech of Positive Intent

Use the language of positive intent. If you expect something to happen, you will show your confidence in your words and your tone of voice. You will unconsciously select powerful words because you expect to succeed. For example, look at some of these power phrases:

- Instead of "I'm only the secretary," say "I am the secretary; I handle other matters. Your question is better answered by . . . ."
- Instead of "I'm not really sure," reply "I don't have that information. I'll be glad to research it and get back to you by . . . ."
- Say "I can," not "I can't."
- Respond "I will," not "I'll try." Eliminate the word "try" from your vocabulary. It offers no commitment. It means, "Maybe I will, if I have the time and nothing interferes, then perhaps . . . ."

As you can see, there are many verbal tools available to make your speech more powerful and convincing. Learn to use them effectively. Use direct speech. Be brief. Eliminate waffle and weasel words. Avoid emotion-laden words. Say what you have to say, then be silent. Speak in positive phrases. Although being powerful verbally is an important skill for the straight talker, learning to read and use the language of the nonverbal is a necessary attribute as well. Understanding nonverbal communications is a powerful straight-talking tool.

8
Powerless Verbal Behaviors

When a playwright creates a character, she considers what kind of person the character is. The playwright gives a weak character verbal tics and speech patterns you will recognize from this chapter. That fact shows how the following word choices and verbal mannerisms rob speech of power.

Words and Phrases to Avoid

Avoid phrases like "I'll be honest with you" and "Frankly." Weren't you being honest with them before? The implied statement is "Up until now, I've been lying to you, but from now on, I'm going to tell you the truth." People use these terms when they speak without thinking. They are the same as saying, "I am not a crook." They provoke suspicion. Other bad speech habits which take away power include ahs, umms, ers, you knows and you know what I means.

Avoid apologizing for things beyond your control. If you're not guilty, don't apologize. One such example is, "I'm sorry it rained for the company picnic." You didn't cause it to rain. You can show your empathy with "It's too bad the company picnic was rained out."

On the other hand, avoid sounding over-confident. A self-centered tone may be irritating and cause others to ignore your message. Do not say, "Naturally, you'll agree with my assessment." Instead, simply use facts by saying, "My assessment of . . . shows . . . ."

Avoid add-on questions such as "John is here, isn't he?"

Qualifiers

Avoid qualifying phrases that dilute the power of your statement, such as, "I may not know much about this, it's just my opinion, but I think the solution may be to adopt Ken's idea." These hedging statements convey self-doubt. They make you sound hesitant and unsure. A simple, more direct, more powerful phrase would be, "We should adopt Ken's idea."

Other qualifying words that add uncertainty are "kind of," "sort of," "just," "really" and "little." More authoritative than "I just wanted to say" is "I want to say," or even better, simply say it. Instead of "I'm really excited about . . ." say, "I'm excited about . . . ." Constantly using the word "really" makes you sound powerless.

Once, years ago, I ruined an outstanding presentation by overusing the word "really." At the end of my speech the audience was wonderfully receptive and gave me a standing ovation. As I stood on stage to warm applause, I said, "I'm really excited to be here. You've really been terrific. I really can't tell you how wonderful this experience has really been." After the third or fourth "really," the applause lessened noticeably and I felt the power drain out of my body. I learned a valuable lesson that day. Simply say, "Thank you for your attention," and accept the applause graciously.

"Little" is another weak word. There's a shop near me that I never go into because it carries only little items. I was there one day, and the sales person showed me the cutest "little" dress, and she suggested that I put a "little" pin on it and she had a "little" hat to go with it. There was a darling "little" purse that would be just adorable with it. Too many "littles" or any other overused word — rob your speech of power. They are empty superlatives, as are cute words like "adorable," "darling" and "wow." Such words don't carry strength.

Never put yourself down by such statements as "This is probably dumb," or "I may be wrong, but . . . ."

Don't run multiple thoughts together with the word "and." It makes you sound like a train out of control. Although women are more likely to do this than men to avoid being interrupted, both sexes have occasional lapses. Keep your statements concise and direct.

Avoid the connecting word "but" where possible. You can frequently replace it with "and." "But" is often a hedge word. Don't say, "Joan is tall, but she's very attractive." The implication is that her height takes away from her appearance. Instead, be positive by saying, "Joan is tall and she's very attractive."

Make the preceding verbal dos and don'ts part of your way of speaking. Examine the words you choose. Incorporate power phrases into your vocabulary and eliminate powerless waffle words and phrases.

Review these verbal choices:

- Use direct statements.
- Use fewer words.
- Express yourself in "I need" statements.
- Use thinking, cerebral words.
- Use "I."
- Paraphrase.
- Choose words that communicate your strength.
- Don't be afraid to be silent.
- Use the language of positive intent.
- Don't use qualifying phrases.
- Never apologize when you are not at fault.
- Avoid add-on questions.
- Avoid empty superlatives.
- Don't put yourself down.
- Eliminate the "and" syndrome.

In addition to the preceding verbal techniques for strengthening your authority, look at the nonverbal tools of the powerful. Now that you have learned your lines it is time to explore how to make your character move powerfully and effectively.

9

Powerful Nonverbal Tools

Nonverbal behavior is the most powerful tool an actor has to portray a character and his or her inner thoughts and feelings. The same is true for persons dealing with real life situations. In this chapter we will examine how to talk straight nonverbally. Nonverbal communication affects many facets of human behavior. An in-depth understanding of this powerful skill will give you an edge in your communications with others. Knowledge of nonverbal behavior will help you to better understand hidden messages. It will add clarity to your communications. It will enable you to be more persuasive in general by responding appropriately to what others tell you nonverbally.

Our four-year-old daughter Dana was in our family room watching a children's show on television. I was at the kitchen sink, washing the dishes. As I washed, Dana rushed into the kitchen. Jumping up and down excitedly, she described a clown she was watching. "Mommy, Mommy!! Quick, come here! There's a funny clown on TV. He has on big floppy shoes and his cheeks have big red circles and he has a round nose . . . Mommy, are you listening to me?"

When she asked me this question, I was doing what so many parents through the ages have done. I was continuing to wash the dishes, looking at the sink instead of my daughter. I threw in an occasional, "Oh, isn't that exciting? Tell me more."

Dana tolerated my lack of interest for as long as she could. Then she stamped her foot, tossed her red head and shouted, "MOMMY, LISTEN TO ME WITH YOUR EYES!" We communicate nonverbally much more than we communicate verbally. As my daughter so brilliantly put it, we can learn a great deal by "listening with our eyes."

In Ken Cooper's *Bodybusiness* and numerous other books, studies by nonverbal communications expert Albert Mehrabian suggest that 55 percent of what we communicate about ourselves is nonverbal. In fact, that same study indicates that 38 percent of communications understanding has to do with the paralingual part of our verbal communications, or how we say what we say: the tone of voice, the speed of speech, silences and pauses. What we say, our actual word choices, makes up only 7 percent of our communications understanding. Nonverbal communication constitutes the rest, a whopping 93 percent.

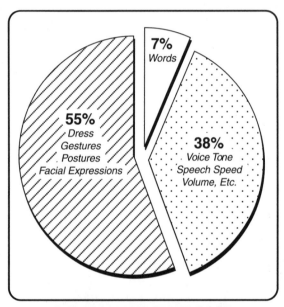

COMMUNICATIONS UNDERSTANDING

Here is another mind-boggling fact. Since body language is for the most part unconscious, it is the most honest form of communication we use. People believe the body if the voice says one thing and the body another.

Nonverbal communication allows people to communicate in numerous subtle and not-so-subtle ways. There is a story about a writer and the movie producer Sam Goldwyn. The writer said, "Mr. Goldwyn, I'm telling you a sensational story — I'm only asking your opinion and you fall asleep!" He replied, "Isn't sleeping an opinion?"

Sleeping during a story is certainly a strong nonverbal clue, usually indicating boredom or disinterest. Unconscious body movements usually have meaning, sometimes unknown even to the person making the movements.

Interpreting nonverbal communication is a complex process. No one piece of behavior says it all or says anything for that matter. But having observed one behavior, you should look for confirming or rejecting signs. Once you have compared several signs, you can draw some conclusions about the other person, the group or even yourself.

People have mixed feelings about most things that are important to them. Nonverbal communication is a person's way of expressing ambivalence. People constantly use double messages in their interpersonal encounters. By reading nonverbal communication clues properly, you will be able to detect shifts in moods and emotional climates and contradictory feelings.

Nonverbal communication is a vital source of feedback about how well your message is getting across. Observing nonverbal clues provides insight into how listeners feel about your message. For instance, a manager asks a programmer if she feels confident in debugging an important program. "Yes, I'm confident," she answers, but her hand tremor and stammer suggest otherwise. Observing this, the manager volunteers to provide assistance in the more difficult portions of the assignment.

Understanding nonverbal communication is like learning a new language. Nonverbal clues are automatic unintentional signals. They don't involve the voluntary nervous system. Since they are not cognitively processed, the messages they communicate are frequently inconsistent with verbally professed statements. People often have mixed emotions or suppressed thoughts about other people and things. Perceptive people can pick up the indicators that body language provides, and then they work to get some communication clarification.

Many psychologists, psychiatrists and social scientists believe that human behavior is motivated. Such motivation can come unconsciously from either positive or negative inner feelings and thoughts. The most common example is the slip of the tongue. Although we excuse ourselves by pretending that the accidental words were totally random, many psychologists argue that the person has made an unconscious association reflecting some hidden basic feeling. When a woman accidentally refers to her husband as "my father" and then blushingly stammers, "I mean my husband," there may be more meaning behind the statement than it seems at first. The slip may have been motivated by some attribute that the woman wished for in her husband that she associated with her father.

An example of motivated nonverbal behavior which may not be apparent is the folded arms. When a person feels threatened in a situation, the automatic folding of arms may be a self-motivated defensive gesture. The behavior's outward signs reflect its motivation. Of course, the folded arm gesture could mean something else entirely. Care needs to be taken in drawing a conclusion from one single clue.

Actors refer to various movements and vocal usages — the way we say what we say — as "stage business." In this examination of the stage business of life, we are going to explore three major categories of nonverbal communication:

- *PARALANGUAGE* or the vocal part of speech and its nuances
- *KINESICS* or the study of the body's physical movements
- *PROXEMICS* or a person's perception of space

Understanding nonverbal communication will give you a better understanding of the people with whom you work or live. It will help you to understand yourself. It will help you to motivate people to become self-empowered. It will help you to communicate far more effectively.

PARALANGUAGE is the vocal part of our speech other than the words themselves: the ers, the ahs, the silences, the unfilled pauses, tone, pitch, rate of speech, volume and voice quality.

• Silence can communicate any number of messages. Silence can represent anger. Communicating is giving of yourself. When you feel angry, you don't want to extend yourself. For example, on occasion I have been known to pout and give my husband the silent treatment. Perhaps that scenario is familiar to you.

• Silence may represent fear. When you are afraid, you pull within yourself and flee from the threat. Silence allows you to become invisible and avoid being a target.

• Silence may mean that a previous message has made a powerful impact. We need time to absorb powerful messages. Perhaps you have left the theater after a particularly moving play and not spoken to your partner during the entire drive home.

• Message emphasizers are the sounds of throat clearing, coughing and ah-humphing. "Er," "ah-um" sounds give one thinking time. Harumphs often occur when the conversation is getting into a sensitive area or we have an overpowering need to say something.

• Tone of voice includes the quality of your voice and other emotion indicators. I'm sure you have known of the following situation or maybe have been in it yourself. A woman calls home, detects something in the tone of voice from her husband, asks if anything is wrong and gets in reply, "Oh, nothing!" Until she gets home and discovers what the "Oh, nothing!" means, the caller will feel uneasy. Simply by emphasizing a different word each time, we can give many meanings to the following sentence:

"I did not tell Doris to go." **Someone else did.**
"I did **not** tell Doris to go." **I'm positive I didn't say it.**
"I did not **tell** Doris to go." **Perhaps I merely suggested or implied it.**
"I did not tell **Doris** to go." **Maybe I told someone else.**
"I did not tell Doris to **go**." **Perhaps she was to stay.**

Sometimes our words and our tones have opposite meanings. Now compare what is said with the way in which it is said.

annoyed: "Of course, I love you! How many times do I have to tell you?"

angry: "Damn it, I'm **not** angry! When I'm angry, I swear!"

sarcastic: "Take the garbage out? I **love** to take the garbage out!"

Without tone, words have little meaning. Tone is the color of speech.

• Pitch represents tonal level. Lower pitch levels are richer and deeper in color and more pleasing to the ear. Thus they are more powerful. On the positive side, higher tonal levels can convey great cheerfulness and excitement. Negatively they can reflect weakness or fear. Examples of women with easily recognizable lower-pitched voices are Lucille Ball and Patricia Neal.

• Timbre is a voice's changing qualities: softness, smoothness, brittleness. Gruff or harsh vocal sounds may communicate an unintentional hostility or aggression. On the other hand, silky-smooth tones might disguise those same qualities.

• Rate of speech is another paralingual aspect of speech. In the words of Hamlet, "Speak the speech, I pray you, as I pronounced it to you, trippingly on the tongue." Speaking too slowly or too quickly creates a negative response. Speaking too fast makes you sound out of control. Of course, don't speak so slowly that people fall asleep before you finish your thought. An effective rate of speech is between one-hundred-forty and one-hundred-sixty words per minute.

Time yourself while reading the following passage out loud. If you can read it in one minute, you are reading at one-hundred-forty to one-hundred-sixty words per minute.

Listenable Rate of Speech

As a representative of your organization, it is important that you speak clearly. That means that you must articulate. It also means that you must speak so that you can be understood. Although there is no set rate of speech, most expert speakers talk at between one-hundred-forty and one-hundred-sixty words per minute. That is a good speed for verbal communication. It is not too fast to be understood. It does not give the listener the impression that you are under pressure nor is it too slow. The one-hundred-sixty word rate adds an element of dignity to your voice. The one-hundred-sixty word rate also gives a sound image to the caller that establishes both you and your company as efficient and well-organized. To give the caller the kind of impression of yourself and your company that you wish, speak correctly, speak at one-hundred-sixty — that's one-hundred-sixty words per minute.

Speed of speech varies tremendously from one part of the country to another. On a hectic day, a Wall Street stock broker may get up to two-hundred words per minute. Someone from a sleepy town in the South on a lazy Sunday afternoon may seem to take an infinite amount of time getting thoughts out. Matching the other person's speed of speech is a useful tool in sales. The implication is that you are just like him or her and have something in common. In an emergency situation, you tend to speak fast. If you are bored or sleepy, you slow down.

• Volume in our speech communicates directly. Extreme loudness creates an unfavorable response in the listener. Loud voices are often equated with bullying, blustering personalities. Too much volume makes you sound pushy and intimidating. As a listener, be careful about making a judgment. The person speaking loudly could be hard of hearing. Conversely, people are often irritated by those who speak too softly. Soft voices don't command respect or attention. Softness of speech may create an impression of meekness and insecurity.

• Voice quality reflects emotion. Is there anxiety in your voice? Remember that listeners tense their bodies in response to vocal tension. If there's strain in your voice, those to whom you're talking will be less relaxed. If you are not breathing from the diaphragm, your voice will have a breathy quality and it will tire quickly. Good breath control is essential. Breathe from the diaphragm rather than the upper part of the chest area. This simple technique will help you project confidence.

To discover how you are breathing, lie on the floor on your back. Place a book on the upper part of your stomach, near your last rib, and breathe. If the book doesn't move but your upper chest area does, you are not breathing properly for good voice quality and breath control.

If your voice is too high or too nasal, open your mouth for all of the vowel sounds. It's difficult to sound nasal when you concentrate on the vowels, not the consonants.

Another technique that I use when getting in front of an audience is the "Umm, hmm" exercise. As I walk up the aisle, I will say to myself mentally, "Umm, hmm . . . umm, hmm." The "umm" is a higher hum and the "hmm" is a lower hum. Then I will simply start speaking on the lower second "hmm" sound.

Women's voices often have higher pitches than men's. There is a physiological reason: women's vocal cords are shaped differently. The fact remains that a lower pitch carries more authority. Think of some of the national women newscasters on television — Diane Sawyer and Cokie Roberts. It is particularly important for women to learn to speak in their lower vocal registers.

KINESICS is the study of the body's physical movements: gestures, facial expressions and postures. I can't promise you that understanding body language will make you rich, sexy or charming, but I guarantee you that correctly reading silent signals will make you a better communicator and a more understanding human being. However, be aware that while some body language is clearly understandable, there are many gray areas where there could be several interpretations. You cannot *not* communicate. Each of us is a transmitter that can't be shut off. We are all constantly sending nonverbal clues. This fact means there is a constant source of information available about ourselves and other people. If you can detect these signals, you'll be more aware of how others think and feel, and you'll be better able to respond to their behavior.

According to legend, President Roosevelt, a firm believer in nonverbal communication, decided to have some fun one evening. Each person came up and shook hands with him and said, "Good evening, Mr. President, and how are you, sir?" He responded warmly with a pleasant smile and a firm handshake, "I'm fine, thank you, I just murdered my mother-in-law." Not one person reacted to his comment! It's doubtful they even heard it. A friend confided to me that for years when asked how she was, she replied, "I'm exonerated." Only one person ever questioned her comment. Try it for fun and see what results you get.

People believe body language even when the words contradict it. Body language transmits feelings; verbal communication transmits words and thoughts. At times understanding the wants and feelings of others is far more important than understanding their words. For example, did you know that the pupils of our eyes communicate? When we are excited or particularly interested in something, the pupils of our eyes increase in size. A good salesperson can increase profits by being aware of pupil dilation!

Edward Hall, a teacher of nonverbal communication, tells of being in a Middle East bazaar where he noted that an Arab merchant insisted that a customer buy a piece of jewelry to which the shopper had been paying very little attention.

However, the vendor had been watching the pupils of the buyer's eyes, had noticed them becoming larger on seeing a particular bracelet and had known which piece of jewelry the buyer really wanted. The customer bought the bracelet!

People don't usually pay attention to body language until a speaker and his body start sending different messages. One of the strongest power signals you can use is to be consistently congruent with your body language cues and what you are saying.

• Posture communicates emotion. Actors are taught that there are two body postures: rising/approaching and sinking/withdrawing. Rising energy is reflected in a lift of the body, ebbing energy in a drooping body. Upward movement is associated with life: a growing plant, a young child, a person of vigor. Downward movement is related to death, the sick, the weary, the discouraged.

This fundamental rising/sinking action is usually motivated by our inner feelings and emotions. However, it's possible to change an inner feeling by changing our outward bodily appearance. On a day when you're feeling depressed, put a spring in your gait, quicken your step, lift your stomach, chest and rib cage, hold your head erect and smile. This positive physical action will most likely help you feel less dejected. Excellent posture suggests power. Even from a wheelchair, President Roosevelt projected power with his erect carriage and jutting chin.

Generally speaking, people who walk rapidly and swing their arms freely tend to be goal-oriented. When people habitually walk with hands in pockets, they tend to be critical and secretive. When people feel depressed, they shuffle along with their hands in their pockets and seldom look where they are going, making it difficult for them to be goal-oriented.

Stooped or bowed shoulders usually mean something negative. One could be afraid, submissive, guilty or self-conscious. Raised shoulders denote fear or tension. Squared shoulders suggest strength or responsibility.

You already know a great deal about body postures. If you observe someone in a phone booth, talking on the phone, you can probably guess to whom they are speaking simply by observing their bodily posture. If one is talking to a supervisor, the posture is more erect. A conversation with a spouse creates a more relaxed, open, even slouched posture, unless there is an argument in progress, in which case the posture would show tension. When speaking to a lover, one shuts out the rest of the world.

When two people adopt similar sitting positions, mirror images, the nonverbal message communicates harmony and agreement. The nonverbal statement is, "I think like you" or "I'm with you." Any abrupt postural shift during the encounter means that the communication flow has altered and a change in thinking has occurred.

Leaning forward reflects intensity, interest in the other person and confidence in yourself. This is a particularly important nonverbal cue for straight talk.

• Gestures are fascinating and have many different meanings depending on the circumstances surrounding the situation. It is unwise to base a decision on a person's personality by interpreting just one of his or her gestures.

The hand-to-hairline gesture often means "You're getting in my hair" or "I'm getting hot under the collar!" As you can see, many phrases in the English language are associated with body-language situations. However, the hand-to-hairline gesture can also represent a flirtatious, preening signal, a nervous gesture or a self-repair sign. It is only when a number of gestures fit together that a complete picture evolves. Gestures are often lumped together in what is called clusters. Each gesture is like a word in a language. It's only when those words fit together to form sentences that accurate interpretations can be made.

The hand gesture is the basic form of human expression and a true index of the mind. Hand-gesture meanings vary tremendously from culture to culture. One salesperson traveling in a distant land used the "thumb-touching-index-finger" sign known in the United States to mean "Everything is O.K.!" He was in for a surprise. In that country this particular signal had the most obscene meaning you can imagine.

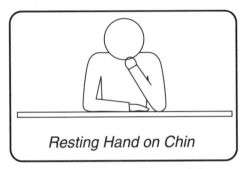

Resting Hand on Chin

CONTEMPLATION

Here are a few diagrams of gestures and their usual meanings. Resting your hand on your chin suggests contemplation.

A common sign of anxiety is hand-wringing, as in the diagram titled **MEEKNESS - ANXIETY.** The well-known character Uriah Heep from Dicken's *David Copperfield* shows meekness with this gesture.

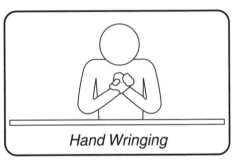

Hand Wringing

MEEKNESS - ANXIETY

Steepling

CONFIDENCE

Making a steeple of your fingers communicates confidence — even smugness, egotism or pride. Many authority figures like doctors, managers and priests use the steepling gesture.

Clasping your hands behind your head also suggests authority. Again, this gesture is seen frequently in managers and bosses.

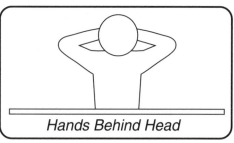
Hands Behind Head

AUTHORITY

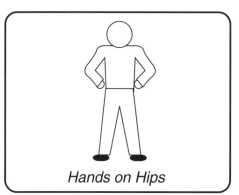
Hands on Hips

POWER - AGGRESSION

Hands on hips with feet spread apart indicates defiance or aggression. It also can be seen as someone making a power play.

The movement most readily associated with sincerity and openness is open hands. Straight talkers use this gesture frequently.

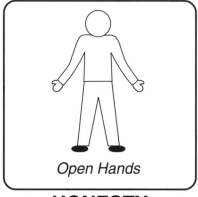
Open Hands

HONESTY

People often assume that crossing your arms in front of your chest is a defensive gesture. It often is . . . but it can have many other meanings. Making a judgment based on a single gesture can be hazardous. Standing with the arms crossed is more comfortable than many other attitudes. It can mean "I'm cold!" and that the person is trying to hold in warmth. It can be an attempt to respect another's personal space. For a woman, crossed arms can mean self-consciousness about her breasts. Beware of judging anyone's movements based on a single gesture. Look for clusters of gestures when reading body language.

• Handshaking is an art. According to C. A. Bartol in a nineteenth century sermon, *The Rising Faith*, "There is a hand that hath not heart in it; there is a claw or paw, a flipper or fin, a bit of wet cloth to take hold of, a piece of unbaked dough, a cold clammy thing we recoil from or greedily clutch with the heat of sin, which we drop as a burning coal."

A person who extends only the four fingers of the hand to be shaken is often reticent and standoffish. Then there is the handshake in which the other person's hand is on top, palm down, forcing you to turn your palm upwards. The person on top has a very dominant handshake; he or she may be out for your job — or your wife or husband. On the other hand, if the dominant position handshaker is a woman, it might simply be a feminine gesture left over from the days when a man kissed a woman's extended hand. The handshake in which the shaker envelopes both of your hands with both of his or hers is known as the politician's shake. It is meant to show warmth and friendliness. It can be sincere or convey great insincerity. Only further in-depth observation will tell the truth.

Be careful about judging someone based on their flaccid, dead fish handshake. There may be mitigating circumstances. Maybe he has arthritis. Perhaps she is an athlete or very strong person who is concerned about hurting your hand. Musicians, surgeons and artists may be protective of their hands.

As a rule, match the pressure used by the other handshaker. Also, as you shake hands with someone, look into her eyes and try to remember their color. This direct eye contact occurring simultaneously with the handshake communicates an honest desire to meet the person.

A proper handshake can make a person much more willing to listen to you. Learn all the nuances of this powerful straight talk tool.

• Facial expressions are important tools for straight talk. When trying to persuade someone, pay particular attention to his or her eyes. Casting a glance upward and rapidly blinking eyelids can mean the person is considering your proposition seriously. If he looks you straight in the eye in a pleasant manner without trying to stare you down, then he is most probably interested. If the person refuses to look at you directly or drops her eyes, hence the expression shifty-eyed, beware — it is possible they will be shifty in their verbal communications as well. Of course, they may be shy or hard of hearing — there could be any number of other explanations. Make judgments only after observing a number of nonverbal clues that all point in the same direction.

Body language varies greatly from culture to culture. In many cultures direct eye contact is offensive; it is often read as a sign of respect to drop one's eyes. Take all of this into consideration when making judgments based on nonverbal cues.

When a person is trying to remember something, she will raise her brows, as if trying to see it. When an individual rejects an idea, he will close his eyes. Once the idea is accepted or understood, the head will nod affirmatively and then the eyes will open wide.

• Smiling is one of the most universally-understood pieces of body language. A smile usually says, "I like you." A smile can be a wonderful source of communication, or it can be a mask that prevents communication. If someone smiles in response to any and every occasion, that smile is likely a mask that hides true feelings and gives that person a chance to collect her thoughts and gain control. President Carter smiled his way through several tense, confrontational moments on television.

Smile when pleased, not to please. Smiling inappropriately or continuously can result in not being taken seriously. A good example of this is evangelist Jim Bakker.

• Head tilting can be significant. Rotating your head upward can be an attempt to claim superiority. This behavior is best exemplified by William Buckley Jr. Rotating your head downward suggests submission or "hanging your head in shame." Tilting your head away during a discussion can indicate disagreement. Tilting your head toward the speaker communicates careful attention and thus agreement.

• Props such as eyeglasses can be effective communication tools. One eyeglasses gesture that causes a negative emotional reaction on others is dropping the glasses on the bridge of the nose and peering over them. Putting the earpiece of the glasses' frame in your mouth can help you to gain time. After all, it is difficult to speak in this position! Taking your glasses off to clean them is another stalling measure.

Pipe smokers are often accused of taking a great deal of time to make up their minds. Decisions can be put off while they fill pipes, tap them and light them.

A cigarette, cigar or pencil becomes an extension of whatever gesture one is making. Because it adds actual physical length to the movement, that gesture takes on significance.

Pointing a finger at someone is often read as aggressive. Therefore, pointing forcefully while holding a long object like a cigarette, cigar or pencil carries an even stronger aggressive meaning.

• Touching is basic communication. Some people are touchers and others are not. Before you touch someone, be absolutely sure that she or he wishes to be touched. If there is no interest in it, DO NOT TOUCH HIM OR HER. There is no worse way to turn someone off than by touching someone who hates being touched.

• Body language provides valuable nonverbal clues. Attempting to persuade people is a difficult task, because the people being persuaded are usually on guard — cautious about anything they say for fear of committing themselves. Because of their efforts to conceal their feelings, they are usually more articulate nonverbally than under ordinary circumstances. Occasionally they reveal a positive decision even though they don't speak a word.

The strongest communication clue that a person has made up her or his mind is gentle stroking of the chin with thumb and forefinger. Usually this is accompanied by a slightly relaxed smile. When a decision is made, tension disappears and the lips curl up a bit. When this happens, the sale is made and the deal can be closed. Seize the moment of opportunity. Go for the close.

Once in a while the salesperson misses this moment and continues selling after the sale is made — to the point where the prospect reverses the decision. A person who continues persuading after the prospect has made a decision is similar to a runner who has won a race and broken through the ribbon, but continues running until he collapses.

PROXEMICS is use of space in communicating with others. Early in my career I wore a dress with a slight train and dolman sleeves to a black-tie affair. I was in deep conversation with a short woman who was standing on the floor in front of me. She was looking up at me. I was standing on a step, framed by a door with arms poised high against the door jamb, allowing my bat-wing sleeves and my almost six feet of height to consume most of the space in the doorway. Suddenly she took two steps backward and said, "You are terrifying me!"

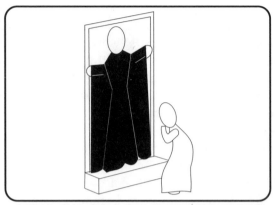

USE OF SPACE INTIMIDATES

I now know that I was unwittingly intimidating her by the way in which I was using space. Proxemics has to do with how people fill space. Tallness and shortness are proxemic principles and involve vertical space use. Space is used by people, gestures, furniture, things or buildings. The way space is used sends powerful proxemic messages. In the above instance, space was filled in several ways. My height was a factor. The long dress with bat-wing sleeves and train used a lot of space. The fact that I was standing on a step accentuated my tallness. Finally the door frame acted as an *italics* surrounding the entire picture, creating an impression of massive use of space.

The distance we maintain with others — our use of space — communicates our feelings toward them. This distance we maintain is called our territorial space. Since the beginning of time, animals — people included — have needed to mark their territories. We all know how dogs mark their territory. Human beings mark territory too — thankfully, in a different way.

There should be little question that your office belongs to you. Your stamp is on it as surely as if you had branded it. If you chose your furniture, then it certainly has your look. What you choose to put on walls, the doodads you scatter about, your nameplate and the selection of books on the shelves all mark the office as **yours.** Even your degree of messiness or neatness speaks volumes. A cluttered office reflects one kind of personality; a neat office another. Both mark the space as your own.

My office is a perfect example. I am able to juggle many projects at one time. Therefore, my desk is often covered with many separate piles of paper. When I receive a phone call regarding a specific project, in most cases I can put my hands on it immediately. On the other hand, a friend of mine who is a time-management expert has a desk top totally devoid of objects except for his current work effort.

One wall of my office is covered with plaques, pictures and honors I have received. Another wall has a wide picture window with bookcases on either side. Business books reflecting my field of interest are packed on the shelves like sardines. Another wall has a large, tall piece of furniture, a credenza with many shelves and file drawers that also house an extensive cassette collection. The dark woods and earthy tones of my office furnishings and walls bespeak my need to be surrounded by warm colors while I work. There are personal items all around the room, including a picture of me, President Clinton and the National Speakers Association Board of Directors during our visit to the White House.

• Space is related to status. Public-relations gurus understand the concept of bigger is always better. The more space filled, the higher the status. Filling more space with a bigger version is perceived by people as being more valuable or prestigious. Advertisements shout **GIANT SIZE,** the big screen and movie extravaganza. A large shopping center is more impressive than a small mall. Homes with large acreage are more desirable than those with small lots. Skyscrapers are more awe-inspiring than a single-story building.

Office size and furnishings are usually indicative of status. A bigger office that uses more space is perceived as better than a smaller one. A bigger desk is more impressive than a smaller and so on. As you rise within a company, one of the perks is often a bigger office, sometimes with a corner arrangement and view.

You can put some of these space principles to work for your next meeting. As room size gets larger and the space per participant increases, participation goes down. If you want a meeting with lots of interaction, put a lot of people in a small meeting room. If you wish to reduce conflict, provide more space.

Many years ago I knew a top executive with a major nationwide corporation headquartered in St. Louis. His office was enormous with a giant picture window overlooking downtown St. Louis and the Mississippi River. A six-feet, four-inches tall friend of mine, Don, described to me the power of being in this man's office during an interview.

The executive's massive chair and desk were placed in front of the picture window in such a way that, when this over six-feet tall CEO was seated, the sunlight coming through the window often seemed to cast a halo around his head. The desk was totally clear of objects. On the other side of the desk was a low, plush chair.

Upon being asked to sit in the low chair, Don seemed to sink forever and found himself looking up for the first time in his life into the face of a halo-enshrouded, god-like figure of a man. Knowing this executive as I do and knowing his great love of and need for power and status, no one can convince me that his office, the size of the desk, the desk and chair placements were accidents. The clean desk nonverbally stated that "I don't have to dig through papers myself. I have assistants who keep track of things for me."

• Territorial research has determined that we have four zones of territorial space: **intimate** from physical contact to approximately two feet, **personal** from two feet to four feet, **social** from four feet to twelve feet and **public** from twelve feet to sight and hearing limits.

Picture an invisible circle surrounding your body. When your territorial space-bubble is violated in some way, invaded by someone to whom you have not given permission, you become uncomfortable. Have you ever felt corralled at a party when someone is leaning over you in such a way that you can smell the onions he had for lunch? He has invaded your personal space.

For the most part, people from other countries have smaller intimate zones than Americans. Even within this country, different people have different intimate zones. This is one reason we get into difficulty and create misunderstandings. In your day-to-day dealings, if a person takes a subtle step backwards when you are standing and talking to him, you are probably encroaching on his personal space. When you notice someone backing away, take a subtle step backwards. Police often use body-space invasion when dealing with criminals; it is a great intimidating tactic. People reserve intimate space for lovers, children and close friends — those to whom they mentally give permission.

People who know each other can stand within each other's personal space. A group congregating around the coffee machine in a work setting is an example of people interacting within personal space.

We all have need for social space. A phrase in our language that reflects this need is "keeping at arm's length." You can frequently tell relationships by observing the way people use social space. The following diagrams illustrate examples of controlling territorial space and reading body stances.

The diagram titled **NATURAL** and the diagram titled **INVADING SPACE** are top views of two people assuming similar stances. However, in **INVADING SPACE** the person standing over the shoulder of the other is too close for comfort, unless it is a loved one, child or close personal friend. In **NATURAL** the person facing forward does not feel threatened by the person slightly behind and to the side of her. The other is not close enough to invade her space.

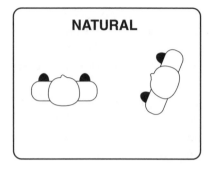

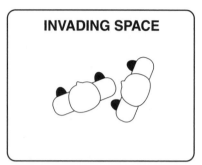

With **IMPARTIAL** the two people are standing side by side as in an elevator. Their body language postures are neutral and not sending any messages to each other. The people depicted in **PROTECTED** are in body positions closed off from each other. They feel safe and secure, not vulnerable to each other.

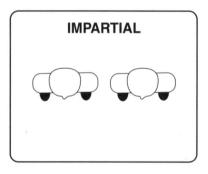

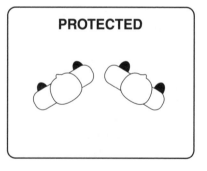

One doesn't have to take much time to figure out who is in charge in the diagram titled **EMPLOYER.** The three people forming a semi-circle are giving space and power to the person centered and standing apart. In **EXCLUSIVE** the person standing to the side is an outsider to this group. The circle is closed, not allowing admittance.

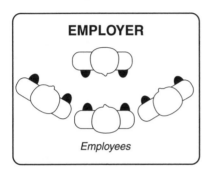 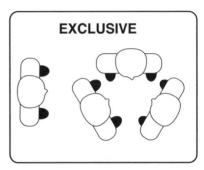

Public space is for strangers. We have no interest in associating with them. Our preference is to maintain a distance of at least twelve feet or more between us.

Public space behavior is fascinating. In China, for instance, where there is very little space afforded per person because of the large population, people often do exercises on the street rather than in their homes. The outdoors provide more of a feeling of space. Psychologically, this group has learned to remove the teeming crowds from their reality. They exercise as if the people milling about them don't exist. It isn't always possible in today's crowded world to maintain a public space, but people will attempt to do this. If a lunch table is filled to capacity and two or three people leave the table, those left will usually spread out to consume the space.

To see how public space functions, try an experiment. In a lunchroom setting, if you see a lone person seated at a round table for five, choose the seat right next to that person. My prediction is that she will move the chair, plate, knife and fork farther away from you in an attempt to maintain a public space. You have broken a proxemics rule and invaded her territorial space.

Sitting in the middle of a two-person bench marks the entire bench as your territory. Many people choose to do this because it helps them to maintain their public spatial need. You might get some irritated looks, but few people will interfere. Sitting on the end of the bench advertises a recognition that the other end of the bench is available for others. If this is the only bench available, my guess is that someone will end up sitting next to you. If there are other bench choices, people will choose an empty bench rather than joining you on yours, even though there may be plenty of room.

• Height and status demand attention. In nonverbal communication, taller is more impressive whether you are talking people, furniture or buildings. The more space used, including vertical use of space, the higher is the perception of status. A tall person — a person using a lot of vertical space — is often associated with success and is perceived as powerful. Very few presidents of the United States have been under five-feet, ten-inches tall. If other factors are equal, research indicates that men in the six-feet, two-inches and over range receive up to 12 percent higher salaries than others in similar positions. The best way to overcome this seeming inequity for a short person is to become superior in ability to others. Competence serves to equalize a height differentiation. Short people can also project a powerful image by carrying themselves with excellent, relaxed posture, choosing well-tailored, expensive clothes and showing a level of confidence.

My first leading role in college was in Shaw's *Heartbreak House*, playing the part of Hesione Hushabye, a strong woman character. I am sure that one of the main reasons that I won the role is my almost six feet of height. I was costumed in a floor-length vibrant red dress, a color which increased the illusion of space. With all the other characters on stage in dull colors, it was hard to take your eyes off my character. I was directed to make large, sweeping gestures, take wide strides and stand majestically — to use space. The other characters were always directed to keep space between us, thus giving my character power through use of space.

I usually find being tall advantageous. Occasionally I meet a short person who I sense is bothered by his shortness. The fact that I tower over him puts a strain on our relationship. In this situation I make it a point to sit down as soon as possible. This equalizes the height differentiation. You can stay even with a tall person and prevent being dominated by keeping a public space of twelve feet or more. Talking from a doorway or sitting at opposite ends of the table can make the odds more even.

If you are tall, you can gain control by moving closer to the person you wish to dominate. If you are short, stay farther away from taller people to avoid being overpowered. An alternative for the short person is to use the drill-sergeant approach. This is not effective if your ultimate goal is to build a lasting relationship.

If you are small or slight, you can minimize this by maximizing your environment. Get a massive desk and high-backed, heavy office chairs. Surround yourself with big paintings and large bookshelves.

• Spatial relationships are critical in meetings. Notice in meetings how people unconsciously use proxemic principles. Where you sit is extremely important. People have been vying for status through seating positions through the ages. Look at the time it took to decide on the seating arrangements for the Paris Peace Talks at the end of the Vietnam War. King Arthur used a proxemic principle by requesting a round table. When all the knights were seated, they had equal influence.

Observe the seating at a conference table. Usually, if it is rectangular in shape, the person in charge takes one end of the table. The opposite seat is often taken by a person who wants to be in charge. If there is a choice of seats, the center ones frequently go to people in competition with each other. This competition can be friendly or unfriendly. The personalities of these people are often curious and aggressive. They want to be positioned where they have a visual advantage around the table or are facing off with others across from them.

If you are in charge of the meeting, consider sitting in the middle of the long side of the table that is facing the doorway entrance. You will be sending a powerful message. By being closer to everyone, you communicate that you are accessible, like to be involved and want to be in the middle of things. You will also be facing meeting attendees as they come into the room. The movie, *Dave,* illustrates this point. Kevin Kline is hired to impersonate the President of the United States. He chooses to conduct his table meetings in the above manner. As the meeting progresses, the movie audience sees the positive effect Dave's seating choice has on the meeting participants. The attendees sense his power. He persuades competing factions to come around to his way of thinking.

Arrive at meetings early so you can chose a power seat. Offer your own conference room where you can arrange the seating for negotiation sessions. Because you have ownership of the territory, you can select the seating for those coming to your meeting by directing them to chairs. Depending on what you want to accomplish, you can increase your chances of success by using the seat-selection proxemic principles discussed below.

You can direct meetings through seating arrangements. By positioning chairs in a circle, you will encourage relatively equal contributions from all group members. If you arrange chairs in a horseshoe or T, you will focus attention on individuals at the head of the group. Chairs placed side-by-side, theater-style, say nonverbally to participants, "You're here to listen, not talk." Don't be surprised if they merely offer questions or comments, without engaging in discussion.

The following diagrams illustrate various types of interaction that might occur at a desk and define what each communicates.

For a meeting in your office, you sit in your chair behind your desk. If the three people invited to the meeting sit as depicted in Figure I, B will have an advantage over A and C. To lessen that dominance, place A and B at one outside corner of the desk and C at another as in Figure II.

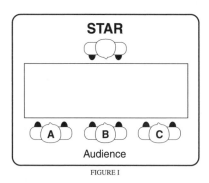

FIGURE I

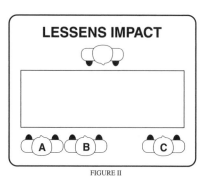

FIGURE II

Two people in a side-by-side arrangement with chairs turned slightly inward toward each other works well for a cooperative undertaking as in Figure III. If you want to create a comfortable conversational area, consider seating your office guest to one side of the desk rather than directly across from you as in Figure IV.

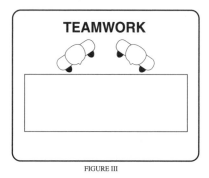

FIGURE III

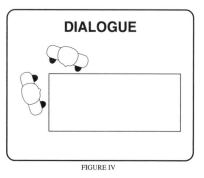

FIGURE IV

When someone is seated across from you as in Figure V, the desk serves as a barrier. Some people prefer this. This arrangement helps you to maintain social space. It can also become more of a competitive setting. Figure VI illustrates a seating arrangement which allows for very little communication. Y would have to move her chair back a few inches to be able to converse freely with X and Z.

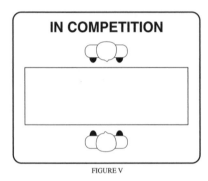

FIGURE V

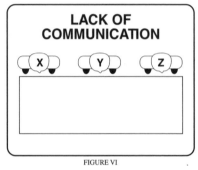

FIGURE VI

You have been using nonverbal communication unconsciously all of your life. To be a powerful straight talker, learn to use nonverbal communication consciously. The words without the paralingual aspects make up only seven percent of communications understanding, according to nonverbal communications expert Albert Mehrabian. Listen to the paralanguage — the stammers, silences, pauses, vocal tics, tone, speed and volume of speech — and put them into a context for understanding. Be aware of other people's postures, gestures and physical expressions and what those nonverbals might mean. Learn to read the body language of others and respond appropriately. Notice how space is used and where people choose to sit. You will be surprised at how you will understand and persuade others with more expertise than ever before.

Special situations may require unique nonverbal and verbal communication techniques. The same is true with theater. Different stage shapes require individual directorial methods. In the next few chapters we will be exploring a few of life's special stage settings like meetings, conflict situations and oral presentations. As with the different theatrical stages, these life settings require unique communication strategies as well.

READING NONVERBAL SIGNALS

Here is a summary of some nonverbal signals and their meanings from Gerhard Gschwandtner's book, *Nonverbal Selling Power*. If you know how to read correctly a person's body language, you will make the right countermoves and have a good chance of creating a desired outcome. If you're unaware of what's happening and how to respond, you can muddle the communications and miss a straight talk opportunity.

1. Dominance, Power
Need to run show. Let them. Don't let them intimidate you, but don't start power struggle either. Never use these gestures yourself in sales situation.

- Hands on hips
- Leg over chair
- Feet on desk
- Hands behind neck
- Steepling
- Large desk, chair larger & higher than guests
- Fingers hooked in belt
- Palm-down handshake

2. Submission, Nervousness
Need reassurance. Try to put them at ease. Don't mirror behaviors or come on too strong.

- Fidgeting
- Hand wringing
- Shifting from side to side
- Self beating
- Constant blinking
- Twitching
- Throat clearing
- Palm-up handshake

3. Disagreement, Anger, Skepticism
Usually reaction to something you've said, verbally or nonverbally. Try to find out why they're unhappy. Don't copy their gestures yourself during a meeting.

- Redness of skin
- Frown
- Crossed arms, legs
- Finger under collar
- Negative shake of head
- Finger-pointing
- Fist
- Turn body away

4. Boredom, Disinterest
Client's reaction to your presentation. Work to regain client's attention. Always look alive to your clients, no matter how bored you are.

- Dead fish handshake
- Blank stare
- Doodle
- Shuffle papers
- Look at door, wristwatch
- Tap feet
- Foot-jiggling
- Drum table

5. Suspicion, Secretiveness, Dishonesty
Almost everyone displays nonverbals when lying, so watch your clients and yourself. Avoid making claims you don't really believe in.

- Nose-touching
- Covering mouth
- Granny glance
- Smirk
- Sideways glance
- Squint eyes
- Ear-pulling while speaking
- Incongruity of gestures

6. Uncertainty, Time Stalls
Clients need break from presentation. Pause, slow down, give client time to gather thoughts and formulate questions.

- Pipe rituals
- Pacing back and forth
- Look of concern or puzzlement
- Head tilted
- Scratch head
- Bite lip
- Clean glasses

7. Evaluation
Client wants to know you are taking his/her comments/objections seriously.

- Glasses in mouth
- Hand gripping chin, index finger up
- Nodding
- Chin-stroking
- Index finger to lips
- Ear turned toward speaker
- Touch tips of temple bar of glasses

8. Confidence, Honesty, Cooperation
You must always exhibit these nonverbals. Concentrate on using this body language as often as possible.

- Lean forward in seat
- Smile
- Vertical handshake
- Sit up in chair
- Jacket open
- Good eye contact
- Open hands
- Feet flat on floor
- Move with speaker's rhythm
- Legs uncrossed

10
Meetings

In theater, various types of stage settings call for different methods of directing. The most common type of stage is the *proscenium* — an open frame in the solid wall of an auditorium which discloses a stage. This is what most people think of when "stage" is mentioned. The *thrust* stage, less common but still frequently used, is a second form of stage setting. This stage platform extends in front of the proscenium arch in either a half-circle or a three-sided square. The most modern stage setting is *theater-in-the-round*. This usually consists of a raised platform, either round or square, with the audience seated in concentric circles around the stage or on all four sides. These separate configurations require special methods of directing. So do the unique life settings in which we find ourselves — meetings, conflict situations and oral presentations.

Here is an example of a special communications challenge for a director of *Speaking of Murder*. The play took place many years ago when I lived in California. The stage was theater-in-the-round. I had the lead part. Auditions were held for the role of the dog. You would think that with all the trained animals in Los Angeles it would be easy to find a superbly trained dog. However, the dog cast in the role was totally undisciplined, although admittedly cute.

With theater-in-the-round, the audience is often within inches of the actors on stage. During one never-to-be-forgotten performance, one man seated in the front row and only a foot away from me and my dog began to make noises to attract the dog. The animal became crazy, running around me in circles with the leash. It took approximately ten minutes for the audience to calm down from their hysterical laughter and for me to untangle myself! Certainly a unique communications situation! The director needed to apply specific techniques to take into consideration this special stage setting.

The same holds true for the various life stage settings in which we find ourselves. Straight-talk behavior in meetings will differ in a number of ways from other communication situations.

Meetings are an intrinsic part of the work day for most people. Learning how to talk straight in a meeting is an important step in increasing your personal power and effectiveness. Knowing where to sit for the most meaningful use of space is a needed business skill. Straight talk in meetings includes knowing about agendas and visual aids. It means considering time constraints and customer priorities. It requires understanding spatial relationships.

I'm sure you have had the experience of attending a meeting that didn't end on time. Have you ever attended a meeting where the participants discussed everything except the purpose for which the meeting was called? In each of these instances, the meeting was not as effective as it could have been.

The following specific steps will improve the quality of your meetings dramatically.

Never call a meeting just to have a meeting.

Have a valid reason for calling the meeting, and define its purpose in advance instead of holding a meeting simply because it is required or to get together to talk. Before the date or hour of the meeting, identify its purpose. Perhaps it is a meeting for the purpose of making an announcement, disseminating information, discussing, decision-making, problem-solving or brainstorming. Call a meeting only if one of the following conditions exists:

- Information is needed from several people simultaneously.
- Complex tasks involving a division of labor need to be performed.
- Activities need to be coordinated.
- The expertise for solving a problem is widely distributed among your employees.

Invite only people who need to be there.

Decide who should attend — not too many or too few. Keep the size of the meeting appropriate to the task. Include employees with the skills, knowledge and authority necessary to address the issue at hand.

Set — and stick to — an agenda.

Distribute a clear agenda well in advance. Prepared attendees participate more actively. Instead of handing out written material at the beginning of the meeting, reports or surveys should be distributed several days prior to the meeting. Follow the agenda closely. Do not go off on tangents.

Be sure that meeting participants learn their roles in advance as well as what they are responsible for contributing. They not only need to know what they are to say, but how long they will have to say it.

Keep the discussions on course. Digression and rambling are big time-wasters and bore attendees. Techniques to help the meeting stay within the topic include: use of visual aids — films, videos, blackboards, flip charts or slide projectors — and the use of brief summaries throughout the meeting. As you conclude each topic, sum up what was discussed and any actions to be taken.

Decide if minutes are necessary, and if so, make arrangements before the meeting for someone to take minutes.

Make sure your room's prepared — not just yourself.

Make adequate, appropriate preparations as you prepare your meeting room. Consider what you want to happen in the meeting. In the nonverbal segment on proxemics, you may recall that we noted, as room size increases, participation goes down. If you want lively interaction and discussion, crowd your people into a small room with no extra chairs. On the other hand, if you want to decrease friction and tension, get a larger meeting room and allow space between the chairs. If you want to encourage confrontation between two people, seat them face-to-face. Side-by-side seating makes disagreement difficult. If you want to dilute confrontation, place someone antagonistic toward the person running the meeting to her right. This position reduces eye contact.

Chair arrangement is important. A conference room setting works well with a small group up to twelve. A U-shaped table is best for approximately twenty. Above that number, consider a classroom-style arrangement. Classroom-style seating works well when people need to write. Theater-style seating is best for large meetings where the format is primarily lecture. Chairs should be comfortable, especially for lengthy meetings.

If possible, select a meeting site free from distractions. Take necessary steps to ensure that unessential interruptions don't occur.

Use visual aids!

Each visual aid should have no more than three major points and should be easy to read with large, clear type. Information on visual aids is explored in great detail in a later presentation skills chapter.

Encourage people who contribute to the meeting.

Support any positive contribution. Avoid inappropriate criticism. Criticism stifles creativity and lessens input from attendees. Begin and end the meeting with an item that unites the group. Create an atmosphere of goodwill.

If you have someone who is consistently long-winded, use a direct approach by saying, "Ellen, we have a lengthy agenda. We need to move on." Another approach is to direct the conversation to another. Say, "I know you also have some ideas on this, Tom. What do you think?" Once the long-winded person has yielded the floor, don't allow him to have it again soon.

Make customer or member concerns your top priority.

Beware of internal power games. It's very easy for a meeting to get out of control when you allow individual pet projects to dominate. Instead, focus on issues, not personalities. Constantly remind the participants of the ultimate goals of the meeting. A meeting that doesn't produce clear, thoughtful solutions is a failed meeting. Ensure the equitable contribution of all participants. Techniques for accomplishing this goal include:

- Having preplanned reports.
- Asking participants to express their opinions.
- Having different participants lead the discussion at different times.
- Listening carefully to each participant.
- Refraining from expressing strong personal opinions about ideas and information.
- Avoiding premature evaluation of contributions.
- Inhibiting participants from expressing strong emotions.
- Minimizing interruptions.

Start on time and end on time.

The mind and body can only absorb so much. Productivity goes down significantly after ninety minutes. Therefore, keep meetings under ninety minutes and end the meeting early if you complete your agenda.

Before adjourning, summarize conclusions and set specific tasks and deadlines by saying, "The proposal regarding the dues increase passed. Mary, will you write an article to that effect and inform our members? That will need to be submitted to the newsletter by no later than March 1. The proposal for the new membership category failed. It needs more work before it can be resubmitted. John, would you chair a New Membership Category Task Force? Have your group come up with some alternatives and present that information at the next Board Meeting."

Take action on the beneficial ideas that are born at the meeting. Too many meetings produce no more than memories of good intentions. To determine if goals were met, do an analysis after every meeting.

A Summary for Running Effective Meetings

The Ineffective Meeting	The Effective Meeting
1. No written agenda	1. Clear agenda distributed in advance
2. Meeting held to talk	2. Meeting purpose identified in advance
3. Written material distributed at meeting start	3. Reports, surveys, distributed in advance
4. Visual aids with too much copy	4. Visual aids to support main points
5. Stupidity, error and misinformation quickly pointed out	5. No inappropriate criticism
6. Internal power games	6. Customer/member concerns top priority
7. Main objective: group consensus	7. Main objective: clear, thoughtful solutions
8. No time limit is set	8. Meetings last under ninety minutes

Always have a valid reason for calling a meeting. Decide who should attend and distribute an agenda in advance. Be sure to follow the agenda closely. Use visual aids and brief summaries to help you stay within the topic. Make careful room arrangements that take into consideration proxemic relationships. Encourage participation. Using the above strategies will make you a powerful straight talker at meetings.

Meetings are fertile grounds for conflict. Being able to handle conflicts effectively is a desirable attribute. Just as meetings require specific communication techniques, so do conflict situations. Sometimes conflict is a necessary step in order to move forward when there are seemingly irreconcilable differences.

11
Conflict Situations

Conflict is an intrinsic part of theater. It is essential for drama. Even the lightest comedies usually have a "boy meets girl, boy loses girl, boy gets girl" theme. So it is with the stage of life. Conflict is an inevitable part of most people's lives. People do not like conflict. Some of us deal with conflict better than others, but it is never something that we enjoy. At best, conflict causes irritation and frustration. At worst, conflict causes health problems, severs relationships and brings productive action to a halt. Changing unproductive behaviors you use in conflict situations will make you a more effective straight talker. In this chapter we'll explore dealing with an angry person, confronting criticism and managing conflict productively.

Dealing With an Angry Person

We have all encountered an angry person. Whether or not we have given that person a reason to be angry, we may wish to stay on good terms with them.

A number of years ago I produced my first audio-cassette album. Everything that could go wrong did. There were numerous misspellings in the blurb, the jacket cover was incorrect and the album was mastered two months late. I took the first few errors in stride. However, when the first shipment of production copies arrived, I discovered an entire box of albums had been ruined because the album covers had bled all over each other. I was livid! I called the producer and screamed at her at the top of my lungs. I was totally out of control! As my conversation with her progressed, I found myself calming down and becoming reasonable. After I finished talking to her, I suddenly realized that she had used my eight-step approach for dealing with an angry person! It had worked.

She listened to my complaints, asked questions and repeated the facts for clear understanding. She said she was sorry to hear that the mistakes had occurred. She apologized with "I'm sorry to hear you've had this problem." She then empathized, "I can certainly understand why you are so angry." She asked my opinion as to how best to solve the problem to my complete satisfaction. Her final comments involved the time frame for a solution and the action steps to be taken. The conversation ended amicably.

That eight-step approach was powerful. A few years later, I hired this producer for another album. I believe it was because she had treated me so well when I was angry at her. Here is the eight-step approach for dealing with an irate person:

1. The first rule is to *listen* to the individual's complaint. She has probably spent some time thinking about and planning what she is going to say. Let the person deliver that planned speech.

2. Learn all aspects of the problem by acting as an adult. In Transactional Analysis, each person has three options that she chooses for dealing with life's situations — the Parent, the Child and the Adult. Parent behavior is judgmental and listens not to the message but the source of the message. Child behavior lashes out at the other with unmitigated rage, full of emotions and with no regard for the effects of expressing them. I was in my Child mode in the above story. Adult behavior takes in factual information. Choose an Adult response. Focus on the content, not the angry tone of voice. Make written notes. Watch your body language. Are your arms and legs crossed? Do you have a frown? Is your own voice cold, biting or unfriendly?

3. Apologize sincerely. This does not mean taking the blame for something that you didn't do. "I'm sorry to hear you've had a problem" is sufficient. Remember, you are dealing with human emotions. Consideration for the other person is important. She feels hurt, and acknowledging that hurt will help calm her down.

4. Empathize. Put yourself in his shoes and try to understand how he might feel by saying, "I can certainly understand that you must feel disappointed right now."
5. Ask questions to solve the problem. Get the information you need.
6. Ask for help. "What would you like to see done?" "I'd like your thoughts."
7. Close your conversation by stating when the problem will be solved and what action will be taken. Be sure to get agreement. "Will this solve the problem?"
8. End the conversation so that the other person will want to do business with you again.

Confronting Criticism

A straight talker avoids the powerless Child responses and acts in a powerful Adult way. Look at the following examples of powerless responses to criticism and their powerful alternatives.

Powerless Response	Powerful Response
• Deny.	• Discuss factually.
• Respond with anger/attack.	• See the good in the criticism.
• Criticize in return, i.e.; "Aren't you a fine one to tell me."	• Unemotionally state your position. "I believe that I'm being misjudged on this point."
• Cry.	• Know when to discount criticism, as when a person has a lot to gain or it isn't true.
• Seek revenge.	• Attempt to solve problem.
• Retreat.	• Admit mistake; fix it.

If you feel that the criticism is unjustified, you have a number of choices. You can:

- Ask for support. "What I need right now is your support, not your criticism."
- Look your critic in the eye. Acknowledge the statement, then move on to your next point or subject.
- Agree with the content as it relates to behavior without allowing it to become a personal attack.
- Change the subject. "This is an inappropriate time. Let's talk about it later."

Handling criticism is not fun for any of us. At times, though, the criticism may be justified. The other's goal may be to help us. Handling criticism well is only one form of conflict resolution. There are many other modes to use for more serious conflicts.

Managing Conflict Effectively

Most responses to conflict fit one or more of five conflict resolution modes:

- Competition
- Avoidance
- Accommodation
- Compromise
- Collaboration

Not every method of conflict is liable to be resolved by every conflict resolution technique. Some techniques are ineffective or even counterproductive in dealing with given types of conflict.

Competition

Competition is a vital element in men's perception of their situation, as established in our chapter on gender communication. From early boyhood to adult, men are taught in subtle and not-so-subtle ways to compete. Competition is a way of life for most men. The desire to win or to be right often drives men to use competition to resolve conflicts. This approach often proves to be a powerless tactic since it results in a win/lose situation. A person who pulls rank and says, "You *have* to do it because I say so," or "That's the way it's going to be," will often get his way. But will the one who has to knuckle under really accept this behavior? Even if she obeys the arbitrary orders, the humiliation involved feeds a desire to get even. It's difficult to build a relationship of trust and respect on the basis of rigid subordination.

A person who uses the competition style is often a bully. She is usually in the Parent mode, using words like "should," "never" and "always." She accuses or blames others. She invades other's personal space. Sarcasm and the use of **you** language is part of this behavior as well. This language puts the other on the defensive.

This conflict-resolution style is appropriate when there is an emergency or crisis. When you shout at young people to keep them from being hit by a car when crossing the street, you want them to understand that there is to be no discussion or argument. It is an appropriate style if losing could undermine your self-respect. If a police officer stops you and insists that you were speeding and gives you a ticket, you may grumble about it, but chances are that, in the final analysis, you will take the ticket and pay it. There may be times when you have to make unpopular decisions. It may be necessary to pull rank if you have information about a situation that you cannot share with others.

How can you react effectively to this mode of conflict resolution? There are a number of approaches you can take. You can tell the truth by saying, "I don't believe I deserve this kind of treatment." With strangers, a comment like "Have I said or done anything to offend you?" or "Are you having a bad day?" allows them to save face. You can paraphrase what the other has said, helping him or her to hear the absurdity of the demand. Finally, you can take the other's position to an illogical extreme. "You're right! Samantha has been doing sloppy work lately. I think she should be fired on the spot! And Jerry made a big mistake last week. We should get rid of him too! In fact, let's just fire the whole office and start with all new people!"

Avoidance

Just as competition is the primary conflict resolution mode for men, avoidance is women's preferred behavior. As little girls, women are socialized to believe that fighting, either verbal or physical, is "unladylike." As little girls become grown women, they shy away from conflict. Like competition, this style is usually win/lose. There are times when it is appropriate. If you are dealing with an overly emotional or irrational person, handling the situation at another time is a good choice. If the issue or relationship doesn't matter to you, then it's appropriate to avoid that conflict.

There are a number of ways to use avoidance behavior. You can laugh and joke so that no serious discussion takes place. You can change the subject. You can look away, fidget or turn your body away from the other.

For the most part, the consequences of using this conflict mode are negative. Because the issue has not been resolved, it doesn't go away; it only festers and grows. Actual physical symptoms can develop. It can cause venting of suppressed anger onto others. A person who comes home after avoiding a conflict and kicks the dog is an example of this sort of displaced anger.

I have been guilty of avoiding a conflict on occasion. Once when my husband called home, I was furious about something he had done. He detected my anger from my tone of voice on the phone. He said, "Is anything wrong?" I answered with icicles dripping from every syllable, "No, nothing!" He made it home from the office in record time to find out what I meant by "nothing." I guess I didn't avoid that one very well after all!

You can make it difficult for others to use this method by letting them know the costs of avoiding the conflict. The conflict will continue, perhaps indefinitely. You can also do some perception-checking, saying something like "I can tell that you're angry. You're speaking in an over-loud voice and your body posture seems tense." Be aware that choosing to address the conflict instead of avoiding can result in a temporary escalation, but clearing the air may be worth it.

Accommodation

The martyr syndrome is typical of this conflict resolution technique. The end result can be either lose/lose or win/win — but it is usually lose/lose. You accommodate by giving in to the other's wishes or demands, even when those desires are contrary to your own. You reveal only your surface needs. You use a lot of speech qualifiers and powerless nonverbal behavior, and agree to go along.

Suppose it is lunchtime, and you, Martha and Charles are trying to select a place to eat. Martha suggests Brennan's and asks how you feel about this restaurant. You respond unenthusiastically, " Oh . . . okay." On hearing your comment, Martha asks, "Is there anything wrong?" You reply, " No, it's fine. It's just that I was sick to my stomach after eating there the last three times. But it's okay. Don't worry about me. I'll manage." Accommodators generally have low self-esteem. When you sublimate your needs, you begin to believe your needs are not important.

One way to prevent others from using this conflict-resolution style is to let them know the consequences of their accommodation. "If you don't have a better suggestion and we go to Brennan's, you realize that chances are good you will be sick again." If the person refuses to choose, then *you* choose; don't allow yourself to feel guilty about any contrary results.

This mode of conflict resolution has many negative consequences. Other people will walk all over you. In turn, you end up resenting them and may try to get even. Your goals are not achieved. Incidentally, parents are often accommodators. If you are a parent, haven't there been times when you wanted that last piece of corn but your child asked for it, so you gave in? As you can see, there are occasions when accommodating is appropriate. If the issue isn't important to you, then accommodation will work. Another occasion on which this mode is appropriate is when you are wrong. In this instance, doing what the other wants and putting aside your wishes will create a win/win situation. Accommodation is also appropriate when your primary goal is maintaining a harmonious relationship.

There are some positive consequences with the next two conflict-resolution modes, compromise and collaboration.

Compromise

Compromise is a win/win situation. You get <u>some</u> of what you want, and so do I. Compromise is an appropriate style when your end goal and that of the other person are not compatible. It can be a temporary solution until a collaborative solution becomes possible. It is an excellent mode to use when the end goal is only moderately important to the parties involved.

When you compromise, acknowledge the other person's perceptions, feelings and wants; maintain direct eye contact and body orientation; and make direct indications that you want to negotiate by saying, for example, "Let's split the difference" or "Can we make a deal?" Compromise creates a harmonious environment and preserves trust and respect. The relationship is maintained or enhanced.

Be aware, though, that the price you pay for the compromise may come back to haunt you later. The real issue may remain unresolved, resulting in future frustration or resentment. Work toward collaboration by acknowledging that the compromise is a temporary solution. Continue with the problem-solving process and aim toward collaboration at some future point. With all conflicts, the ideal outcome is for both parties to win or at least to get part of what they want. Learn to separate people from problems and become a problem solver. Then you will be well on your way to consistently using the straight talk method that works effectively in most situations, collaboration.

Collaboration

The best technique for conflict resolution is collaboration — the classic win/win solution. When you collaborate, you find a way for everyone involved to achieve their goals.

When you truly collaborate, you will use the skills you learned from this book. A straight-talking collaborator will listen and indicate that she is listening by using paraphrasing methods, perception-checking and nonverbal attentiveness skills. The straight-talking collaborator doesn't blame the other. Finally, the straight-talking collaborator speaks in the first person: I need, I want, I feel and I think.

Collaboration is the conflict-resolution mode to use for most conflicts. The only exceptions are identified in the descriptions of other conflict-resolution techniques. Collaborate when both the relationship and the issue are important to you. Collaboration doesn't mix well with the other four conflict-resolution modes. Determine in advance whether or not you really *want* to collaborate.

Use the conflict-resolution mode that works best for the conflict you face. If you can learn to resolve conflict productively, you will become a powerful straight talker.

The ability to present well is also a requirement of the effective straight talker. Oral presentations, like conflict situations, require special techniques for communicating your message effectively.

12
Stage Fright

The world of the theater is not as distant from the world of the business speaker as you might imagine. As with an apprentice actor, the novice business speaker may experience nervousness or stage fright. The experienced business speaker is a good performer. Speaking demands vitality, physical stamina and imagination. So does acting. Speakers must work with the audience and show respect for their knowledge. So must actors. Great speakers feel affection for their audiences. So do great actors.

I have been speaking professionally since 1972. I have been a professional actor for longer than that. Even if you don't want to be a professional speaker, presenting and speaking well are important business skills. Speaking skills will help you to meet your objectives. It will give your career a boost. The confidence gained from speaking effectively will carry over to other areas. Fear of speaking in public can be detrimental to your career.

I became interested in public speaking when I was in high school. By college I had had considerable experience in making presentations. I entered a speech contest in my first year at Washington University and reached the finals. One of the requirements for the final competition was to rewrite our speeches and present the new versions one week later. It was a hectic week. At the time I was managing a dance studio after school and working toward a college scholarship. During that week I spent very little time honing my craft by rehearsing. I thought that a couple of quick run-throughs would cement the information in my mind. Not so! Since I hadn't chosen my topic, I had no prior knowledge of the subject of my speech. When the day of the finals came, I thought that my sketchy preparation would be enough to see me through. I was dismally mistaken.

During the presentation, I allowed my negative self-talk to influence me. Negative self-talk is never constructive; it is destructive, even debilitating. When you say to yourself, "Your mind is going to go blank," guess what? The mind does not know the difference between truth and fiction. It believes anything you tell it. On hearing those awful words, your mind says, "Okay" and promptly goes blank!

This is what happened to me at that critical moment in front of the judges. I could not remember my name, let alone the next part of my speech. My mind was devoid of anything but "They are all looking at me." Deeply embarrassed, I stammered a few words and asked to be excused. I have since learned to program my mind with positive thoughts: "I'm doing great! I'm going to 'wow' them! I'm going to be terrific!" The mind is a wonderful thing. It starts working the minute you are born and never stops . . . until you get up to speak in public.

I made a number of mistakes common among beginning speakers during this debacle. Those mistakes were as follows:

• I had no knowledge of the subject. Know your topic!
• I hadn't rehearsed enough. Practice, practice, practice!
• I allowed negative thoughts to influence me. Think positive!

Later we will look at some relaxation techniques and show-business gimmicks that will help to quell your anxiety. Finally, we will examine the use of humor in speeches — a sure way to dispel your own nervousness.

Just to see where you stand, take this little quiz.

SPEAKING QUIZ

Select the best answer:
1. Is it generally a good idea to open a speech with a joke or funny story?
   A. Yes
   B. No
2. A primary concern of many executives when making a presentation is nervousness. The second biggest worry is:
   A. Holding the audience's attention
   B. Making a good impression
   C. Knowing what to do with their hands
3. Visual aids are an important part of a presentation because:
   A. They give your message a lift.
   B. They make it appear as though you are fully prepared.
   C. They heighten audience retention of your information.
4. When giving a speech or a presentation, you should:
   A. Let your eyes sweep across the audience from side to side.
   B. Look at a person and present one complete thought, then move on to another person and repeat the process.
   C. Focus on a spot in the back of the room.

Compare your responses with the following answers:
1. The answer is B. Use humor only if it involves a personal experience — a joke on yourself or anecdotes and analogies that apply directly to your message. Most people are not effective enough joke-tellers to begin this way. If the joke bombs, it makes it harder for you to get the audience back.

2. The answer is C. Most executives find that they don't know what to do with their hands. It is important that you use gestures to support your words.
3. The answer is C. Although all three answers are valid, C is the best answer. Research shows that 80 percent of what a person remembers is the information gained visually.
4. The answer is B. This is the only real way to keep your audiences' attention.

Most of us are at least a little nervous when we step in front of an audience. Even if you are somewhat experienced, don't you find that you get the jitters occasionally? According to the People's Almanac Presents the *Book of Lists*, fear of speaking in public is more pervasive than fear of dying! If someone says he would rather die than speak in public, he may be telling the truth! However, experiencing nervousness is not all bad. Nervousness is nature's way of getting us ready for what lies ahead. Therefore, you don't want to get rid of nervousness; instead, learn to control it. I have been speaking professionally for over twenty years, but I still have occasional moments of panic. Anxious anticipation is a part of every presentation. What I experience now is **controlled** anxiety.

In one of the first plays in which I had a lead role, a young, inexperienced woman actor was cast as a maid — a two-line part. During rehearsal, she spent an inordinate amount of time asking for directorial advice: "Should I emphasize the word *is* in the line, 'Dinner is served,' or should I emphasize the word *served*? Am I standing right? How should I hold the tray?" She wasted time every rehearsal this way. By the last dress rehearsal she was a basket case. One half-hour before opening night curtain she had not arrived at the theater. When the director called her home, he discovered that she was in the hospital. She was so terrified that her jaw locked in an open position and would not close. It stayed that way for the first three days of the play's run. When she discovered that she had been replaced in the maid's role, the jaw miraculously became mobile again. She had the worst case of stage fright I have ever encountered!

There are four levels of anxiety that speakers experience:

1. Novice speakers feel absolute terror and do everything possible to avoid speaking in public.
2. Intermediate speakers experience some fear but are still able to impart information. They may have a hard time departing from their scripts or fielding questions but they can deliver their speeches.
3. Advanced speakers do a credible job, but once again they may experience some vocal tension and feel butterflies in the stomach.
4. Professional speakers experience butterflies but are able to control them. Professional speakers experience stimulation and adrenalin instead of tension.

Nervousness about speaking comes from three main sources:

- Poor self-perception and low confidence
- Failure to prepare thoroughly
- Unrealistic expectations of perfection

Let's touch upon these, one at a time.

Poor self-perception and low confidence — When delivering a speech, most people burden themselves with negative self-talk, such as "They're going to laugh at me!" "I'll forget something," "I'll go blank!" or "I'll stutter!" The audience will be unaware of your lapse. Have yourself video-taped when speaking. Surprisingly, a video-tape helps you discover strengths — not weaknesses. You will be amazed at how confident you look. Perception is everything! When asked to give a speech, remember that you are chosen because the other party thinks you are the the most qualified person to do it. You are the expert, the authority. There is a reason why you, not someone else, were asked to give the speech.

Many years ago I was asked to present a masters track program for top-level professional speakers at the National

Speakers Association National Convention. The program was called "Theater Techniques for the Platform." At first I was terrified! I thought, "Many of the master-level speakers have been speaking for forty or more years. What can I tell them that they don't already know?" Then I remembered the advice I just gave you. I have been a professional actor all of my adult life. I am a longtime member of Actor's Equity Association and the American Federation of Television and Radio Artists. Very few speakers have these credentials. I have valuable expertise in this field that is useful for speakers. I put together a content-filled program that ended with a standing ovation!

Failure to prepare thoroughly — Nervousness is fear of failure. Before the opening of *Annie Get Your Gun*, someone asked Ethel Merman if she was nervous. She replied, "I know my lines. What is there to be nervous about?" Therein lies the secret of conquering anxiety. Become message-centered and audience-centered, not self-centered. Stop thinking of yourself, and start thinking of your message.

If you are thoroughly prepared, your internal nervousness seldom shows. If you forget something, no one will know unless they have your script. Know your material inside and out. Prepare one hundred fifty percent. Get started immediately. Rehearse, rehearse, rehearse. Talk out loud, and walk around while you practice. Use the same physical energy you plan to use on the day of the program. Do the speech at the same vocal level as if you had an audience. When you believe that you are ready, practice while driving in your car. If the speech is firmly enough entrenched in your mind that you can recite it while concentrating on your driving, you will be able to pull it from your unconscious when you are on the platform. Record yourself on a tape recorder. Listen and take notes. Watch yourself in a mirror. Have yourself videotaped. Learn, word for word, your introduction and conclusion. Then deal with the other main points of your speech in an off-the-cuff way so that it sounds comfortably conversational.

Nervousness is caused by fear of looking ridiculous to others. We look ridiculous if we are not well prepared and if we don't deliver the message well. Eliminate stage fright by preparing your material and yourself thoroughly.

Unrealistic expectations of perfection — Give yourself permission to make mistakes. If you think that by forgetting a word or not emphasizing a phrase you have failed in your presentation, you are wrong. People are not perfect in real life. When you are on stage and speaking, you should be like real life — only just a little bigger. It's more important to know the points you want to make inside and out than to give a word-perfect rendition from the platform.

Remember, you want to be nervous. It can be a positive reaction. When you have totally eliminated nervousness, you're probably dead. Dead people don't make good speakers! You don't want to eliminate the butterflies in your stomach; you want to get them to fly in formation. When that happens, you have converted your stress into platform power.

Show Business Gimmicks to Control Stage Fright

The following are some techniques that actors use to reduce audition anxiety. These physical gimmicks will help control the symptoms of nervousness and turn them into positive energy and power.

1. If your legs quiver, move them. One physiological axiom to remember is that muscles in use can't be tense. If you are backstage, pace, bend and stretch. Shake your arms and legs. If you are out front, take long, deliberate strides as you approach the platform. Stretch your muscles. I know a speaker who, before climbing the stairs to the dais, bends to pick up an imaginary piece of lint and then continues. He is stretching his muscles. When you get behind the lectern, press the balls of

your feet to the floor, then release. It is an isometric exercise. The audience will not be aware of what you are doing. Do this again as you begin your speech.

2. If your hands shake, clasp them together and push and stretch the muscles that control your fingers. Do this before you go on stage while you are still seated in the audience or at the head table.

3. If your chest or body is tight, take deep, slow breaths. Hold the air inside your lungs, then slowly release. This technique gets oxygen into the blood.

4. Backstage before you enter, yawn — enormously — with a full stretch. This is the best relaxation technique of all.

5. To keep the pitch of your voice from rising, try the "umm hmm" exercise. If you are nervous, your vocal cords will tighten and drive your voice up.

6. If your mouth is dry, ask for room-temperature lemon water to get your saliva flowing before you speak. Do not drink ice water. You can accomplish the same thing by running the tip of your tongue across the roof of your mouth. Try it now. The saliva flow begins immediately. To keep your inner lip from sticking to your teeth, put Vaseline® on your teeth a short time before you begin the speech.

7. If you perspire on stage, use foundation powder before going on stage. This works also for men, if you are far enough from the audience that it doesn't show. Don't keep your hands in your pockets. They will sweat even more. Use your hands to gesture. From a practical viewpoint, this will help to keep them dry.

8. Visualize your audience in a positive light. People often treat the audience as an adversary. Realize that the audience is usually on your side. No audience comes to a presentation hoping to be bored by an ineffective speaker. They want you to succeed. View them as your friends. Make them partners. Involve the audience early in your presentation. This will help to relax you and energize them.

9. Psych yourself up. As mentioned a number of times throughout this book, use positive self-talk and avoid negative self-talk. Gymnast Mary Lou Retton was once asked what went through her mind before competitions. She replied, "I look at the audience and say to myself, *Just wait till you see this next one!*"

10. If someone asks a hostile question:
- Avoid an argument or a defense of yourself.
- Stroke the person by offering a genuine compliment.
- Disarm hostile people by finding a grain of truth in what they say.

Relaxation Techniques

To relax prior to a speaking engagement, turn on some soft music and go through the following stress reducers. These techniques require a quiet, at-home place. Get into a comfortable position, sit back, relax and follow these suggestions:
- Close your eyes.
- Tune in to yourself.
- Become aware of your body.
- Become aware of your breathing.
- Feel the air come into your lungs; trace the oxygen through your body until you exhale it.
- Take three, deep slow breaths, and feel your body relax more with each breath.
- Feel your hair. Try to sense the actual spot where the hair enters your scalp.
- Become aware of your hands. Are they dry, cold, tense?
- Tense up your hands. Now relax them.
- Become aware of your little toe. What is it feeling right now? Tighten your toe. Now relax it.
- Become aware of your entire body. Feel the clothes draped around your body. Feel the air around you.

- Tense up your entire body — hold it — make it tighter — hold it — relax — take three deep breaths.
- Tense up your entire body again — hold it — tighter — hold it — tighter — hold it — your tightest — relax and take three deep breaths — relaxing more with each breath.

Use of Humor to Dispel Anxiety

A professional speaker friend of mine asked another professional speaker, "Is it necessary to use humor in your speech?" The other speaker answered, "Only if you want to get paid!" While you may not be a professional speaker, if you add some humor to your presentations, you will enjoy a number of benefits.

Humor, used appropriately, banishes stage fright. Humor grabs the audience's attention. It energizes and revitalizes them — people love to laugh. It actually increases blood circulation and feeds oxygen to the brain. It releases pain-killing endorphins. Finally, it helps your audience to remember your points. However, as the earlier quiz pointed out, if you're not a good joke teller, don't begin with a joke. Instead, use real life stories and experiences that make a point. Make sure your humor is relevant. You can tell a funny story, but if the listeners can't relate it to the point you are making, it won't work well.

One fail-safe technique is self-deprecating humor. Pick on yourself. Here's one scenario I use. My husband Ken accompanied me on a speaking tour. When we returned, my daughter Dana asked him, "What did you have to eat?" Ken answered, "Lots of beef and 7,886 green beans." Dana said, "Quit kidding, Dad. How would you know exactly how many beans you ate?" He replied, "When your mother is speaking, how do you think I occupy my time?"

Here is another example: When I found I was going to speak to such a prestigious audience, I was nervous. I told my husband of my concern. He said, "Don't worry, honey. You don't have to be charming and brilliant all the time — just be yourself."

Look for humor in everyday situations. If someone else laughs, you can be sure it is funny. Be aware. Carry a notebook, and jot down funny things that happen to you during your work day. Go early to meetings. If something happens that makes people laugh, tie it in to your presentation and to the group. Use examples from your audience, but be sure to put them in a good light. The only one you want to make fun of is yourself. If you use personal examples, they don't have to be rolling-in-the-aisles funny. A slight chuckle works well, too. If there is something in your background that connects you to the group, use it. It will make you one of them.

Here is a story I used recently. I was hired to keynote a conference for the National Association of Synagogue Administrators. I found out that they had been reluctant to hire me because I wasn't Jewish. What they didn't know was that I had converted to Judaism right after college. I was indeed Jewish. Here is the way I used that information. I said to the audience of two hundred, "Let me tell you something about my background. I was born in Little Rock, Arkansas, into what is known as a hard-shelled Baptist background. My grandfather was a Baptist minister, and so were a couple of uncles. However, my father was a traveler, a deep thinker and very worldly. For example, I had sixteen years of dance training — a taboo in some sects of the Baptist religion. In college I was still questioning my faith when I met the man who was to become my husband of thirty-eight years. He happened to be Jewish. I became enamored of the Jewish faith and converted. I have belonged to a Temple for some thirty-plus years. I have even taught religious school and helped conduct a service. There is one side effect to all of this. You've heard of *Baptist* guilt? . . . Well, I had twenty years of that. On top of that, add thirty years of *Jewish* guilt. Please understand, whatever it is — I'm guilty . . . It's my fault!" The audience of synagogue administrators loved it! They laughed and applauded. I was immediately welcomed into the fold.

The main thing is to "be in fun." Enjoy yourself. Listen to television for ideas — Leno, Letterman and Rivers. Do *not* use blue humor. Keep it clean.

Have fun stuff you can use. Comic strips are a great source — Cathy, Andy Capp and Sally Forth. There are many humor books on the market. Take a shot at using humor, but don't try to be something that you are not. Sincerity and honesty are more important than humor.

If you do decide to use a joke, here are some guidelines. Try a joke on friends to assess the laugh potential. Always try out new jokes in the middle of your speech. Use the funniest personal story in the first part of your speech. Use body language and pauses to enhance the joke or story. Remember, *you* are your best visual aid.

One technique is to quote famous comedians and use their jokes to make your point. Here are some examples:

- Joey Adams said, "We live in a time when a pizza gets to your house faster than the police." I don't know if I can deliver that fast, but let's get started on our objectives for today.

- Comedian Billy Elmer said, "I'm not fat, I'm overweight due to water retention. Right now I'm retaining Lake Erie." Well, I don't know if you can retain Lake Erie, but I hope I can help you retain the key points of today's training.

- Rodney Dangerfield said, "I have a really dumb dog. I went out last week and bought one of those special dog whistles . . . he won't use it." Unfortunately, that's the way it is with some training. People get it, but they don't use it. We hope to change that today.

It is highly improbable to find the best joke at the last minute. Create and work on a file of jokes you really like. When you need humor for a presentation see if you can use one of your favorites to lift the load or emphasize a point.

Following are some observations from Herb True, Ph.D., CPAE, a veteran presenter and humorist on the lecture circuit, about using story materials, props or jokes that will create a learning atmosphere by making people laugh. Remember that brevity is critical. Nothing kills even good material like unnecessary length.

Practice and work both the setup and the punch line. Don't just keep it short, but speak at a brisk pace, then pause and accelerate into a clear short punch line. Don't fade on the punch line. If you overemphasize anything, make it the important words in the close.

Lend validity to your material by personalizing your story with names, locations and specific activities. Master and time your pauses. Give your audience a chance to visualize the graphic picture and grasp the whole situation.

Allow yourself to think and feel funny. Even risk acting 'silly.' Don't be afraid to show that you enjoy spreading cheer. Exaggeration can be a big part of humor. Use your face and big gestures to paint pictures and get the audience involved.

Keep using your winners. Some people like hearing a really good storyteller tell his best stories again and again. The gift of laughter is a very special gift. Use high-impact humor sandwiches. Tell your audience the point you intend to make, then tell the story or joke to illustrate the point, then repeat the point. Hammer home your message with honest, authentic, believable enthusiasm.

Here are some pointers on what to do if there is a disaster. Have some lines hidden in the recesses of your mind that you can pull out. For example, when you drop something or something falls, say, "I guess that tray of glasses disagreed with my last point." When something breaks, say, "I would fix this, but the only thing I learned in shop class was how to call for estimates!" When the lights go out, try, "I guess I'll have to donate a portion of my fee to the electric company." When the microphone squeals, use, "I'll bet you never heard anyone clear their throat like that before." When the projector light burns out, respond with "This is the first time I've been brighter than my equipment." When someone points out a misspelling, answer, "Oh, I apologize, my word processor had a virus."

When you use humor appropriately, your stage fright will vanish amid the chuckles. Now it is time to organize the presentation.

13
Before You Say a Word

A playwright begins the process of writing a play with a great deal of research that takes place before putting pen to paper. A similar creative, information-gathering process must happen before crafting a presentation.

Step One: Determine the occasion for the speech. It might vary from a few brief remarks at a weekly department meeting to a formal report to a professional committee. It might be a sales presentation to convince a prospect. It might be a full-blown speech to a civic group in the community. For me the occasion varies tremendously from forest rangers in Alaska to cruise ship passengers to bankers in New Hampshire. Obviously, my presentation needs to be different for each of these groups.

Step Two: Determine the objective. What are you trying to accomplish? What do you want the listeners to do when you finish? Is your purpose to inform, to persuade, to entertain, or perhaps a combination of these objectives? Every talk should make one primary point — and only one primary point. Try to reduce the essence of your presentation to a single sentence. Only then should you add more content. Everything else you do should follow these objectives. My single-sentence objective for this chapter is to explore skills and techniques that will help you organize your presentations. Take a moment to think about a recent speech you gave or one that you will be presenting in the future. Reduce it to one primary point.

Step Three: Analyze the audience. Find out in advance where their heads are — demographics, opinions, knowledge level and educational level. What are some methods that you can use to get this information? Find out through phone and personal interviews, pre-program questionnaires, pamphlets and newsletters. Look for audience "hot buttons." The hot buttons that would appeal to a convention of hog-callers would be different for a convention of corporate executives. Keep your listeners in mind. The content, vocabulary and diction you use should be appropriate to them.

Step Four: Select your material. Begin with a search of your own mind. Remember, you are the expert, the person selected to give the presentation. Use statistics, stories and anecdotes. To further flesh it out, read books and surveys. Gather twice as much material as you need, and then select the information to be used based on relevance to your objective and your audience, accuracy and human interest. To get your audience involved, plan question-and-answer periods, exercises, films and humor. To create human interest, use personal stories and create visual imagery.

Step Five: Structure the material. A well-organized presentation will enhance your confidence and help the listeners follow you. Most people retain no more than twenty five percent of what they hear. This means that seventy five percent of what people hear goes in one ear and out the other.

Immediately after the average person has listened to someone talk, he or she remembers only about one-half of what was heard. Within the next eight hours, one-half to one-third of that disappears.

Every presentation should have an introduction, a body and a conclusion. This maxim applies to both a three-minute and a three-hour presentation. There is a well-known saying, "Tell them what you're going to tell them, then tell them, then tell them what you told them."

The introduction should comprise ten percent of the talk. Its purpose is to get attention, to set the mood and to prepare the audience for the topic. The body of the talk should comprise eighty percent of the speech. This is the substance or meat. The last ten percent is for the conclusion. Leave the audience with a call to action or an uplifting motivational moment.

Work on the speech content — the body — first. Then develop the conclusion. Finally, plan the introduction. Use a standard outline with the main points listed, and then add subordinate points under those.

At the end of each point, give a summary, then transition to the next point: "We've had an opportunity to look at how to control anxiety and nervousness. We've explored how to prepare the presentation and organize your message, including selecting and structuring the material. Now let's investigate platform mechanics and the use of visual aids and sound equipment."

Visual Aids

Why use visual aids? There are a number of reasons. First, visual aids help the speaker to feel more confident. Second, they help the audience concentrate. Third, they help the audience to understand and retain your material. Fourth, it tells the audience that you're serious.

You and the props you use are your best visual aids. Six other common visual aids are films, videos, 35mm slides, chalkboards, flip charts and overheads.

Let's begin with films and videos. There are many great films and videos that are available to support almost any message. The advantages of films are that they are usually professionally crafted and easy to use. If you decide on a film, you will need a screen, projector and someone to run it. Films and their necessary equipment can be costly to rent and even more so to buy. For a video, you will need a TV monitor and a VCR. When either a film or video is running, it becomes the star. However, building a program around a film or video can be an effective technique.

Slides are a popular visual-aid choice. You may want to have your slides professionally made. They can be as simple or as elaborate as you like. Slides require a darkened room, which again makes the slides become the star. People came to see you, not your supports. It is awkward to turn the room lights on and off, so chances are you will end up leaving them off, which again, makes the slide the center of attention. However, this visual aid is often preferred for groups of over one hundred persons.

Another visual-aid is the chalkboard. I seldom use a chalkboard. If you are speaking to a small group of under twenty people, a chalkboard allows you to interact with the listeners and get audience participation. You cannot do advance preparation with a chalkboard, and it is not as easy to read as some of the other visual aids.

A flip chart is often a better choice for a small group and an easy one to use. It works particularly well in an interactive situation. If you choose to write on the flip chart in advance, skip a page between each written-on page so that the writing on the underneath page does not show through. Use large, dark pens and practice your writing. Be sure to spell correctly. There is nothing that will embarrass you more than a misspelled word. Keep it simple. Use a pointer. Here are some guidelines: Two-inch lettering for up to thirty feet deep of audience; four-inch lettering for up to sixty feet deep. After that, I suggest you either go to slides or overheads.

Overheads are also called flimsies, acetates, view graphs, vu foils and transparencies. They are portable and can be prepared in advance or be spontaneous. You can write on them as the audience gives feedback. They are visible by up to approximately one hundred people, and they allow the speaker to face the audience. The room lights can be on continuously. This means that there is no distraction with lights being switched on and off. You remain the star of the program. The purpose of a visual aid is to supplement, not replace, the speaker. Always face the audience when you use overheads. If you position the transparency correctly on the projector, it will be displayed correctly on the screen. You can buy frames for transparencies and create them on a laser-jet printer, if you have the proper fonts. Turn the projector on when you want to show an overhead, and shut it off in between. When you use the off switch, the audience's eyes will go to you. When you turn the switch on, their eyes will go to the screen. Keep the overhead simple.

The *reveal* is an excellent method to keep your audience from reading ahead. Use a white sheet of paper between the transparency and what is called the stage — the glass top of the projector — and slide the paper down, uncovering a new line and revealing each new point. Another method is to lay a pencil or a pointer on the transparency at the point that you are discussing.

Another possibility is to use a laser pointer to highlight a line on the screen. Stand to the side of the screen, or move around so that you are not blocking the view of the audience. You will need to focus and position the image carefully before the presentation. Frame your overheads or use one of the framing devices that you can buy so that light does not leak around the overhead. Use six lines or less per visual, six words or less per line.

Color is exciting. If you can use color or clip art or both, the result is more effective. If you frame your transparencies with cardboard, you can actually write notes on the cardboard to help keep you informed of what points you want to make next. Don't use words alone. Use charts, illustrations and cartoons along with the words and title each transparency. You can add impact to your program by filling in the blanks of the transparency as you speak. Use the projector for emphasis. Pause briefly after switching it on to let the audience absorb the information. I always ask that the projector be placed on a wide table rather than the usual small projector stand. This allows ample room for props. Finally, don't begin or end your program with a visual. It kills the human element. Remember that people come to see you, not your slides or your visuals.

Props, Microphones and Such

Don't be afraid to use props. I have used Ben Franklin glasses to play a personality type or magazine covers to illustrate a point. Props add visual appeal. They help to paint pictures in the audience's mind. Props can range from a feathered pen to a cape to chimes — anything that will attract attention or help to clarify your point.

There are other mechanical factors to consider in making your presentation effective. A microphone is useful when you speak to a group of more than twenty people. You can use a microphone to create excellent whispery special effects. A meeting planner once asked my speaker friend Jim Cathcart, CSP, CPAE, if he really needed a mike. In "meeting-planner speak," that means, "I forgot to get a microphone; just project more." Jim told him, "No, I don't need a microphone. I've heard this speech dozens of times. However, your audience needs the microphone so *they* can hear *me*."

I carry my own sound system. I use a cordless lavaliere mike so that my hands can be free, but this is for the more advanced speaker. For people who are uncomfortable having both hands free, a hand-held mike will work better.

Be careful where you place a lapel mike. For men, place it on your tie, not lapel. If you place it on your lapel, the sound is affected when you turn your head. Your voice goes off-mike. Don't place the mike too far from your mouth. Approximately six inches from your mouth is correct. If you place your lapel mike farther than six inches from your mouth, either you will not be heard or you will get feedback when the volume is turned up.

If you use a cord with your mike, ask for a long cord and place the cord in the back of your skirt or trousers and hide it under your jacket so that you don't trip over it as you walk around. Check the sound system with the hotel electrician or sound person *before* your audience comes into the room. The sound system should check out perfectly before you begin the presentation. Test it yourself first for feedback problems by walking around the area in which you are actually going to give your speech. Then have someone else talk into your mike while you check every corner of the room to ensure that you can be heard. Make sure the sound is coming through *all* of the speakers. Beware of speakers in the ceiling, particularly in front of the lectern. Speakers that are *in* the lectern can create feedback if you step in front of them. If batteries are required for the mike, make sure that they are fresh and that you have a spare. You need to be careful about another common problem — p-pops — an exaggerated popping sound that is sometimes heard when there are a number of words in a row that begin with the letter "P." Not long ago I heard a speaker who had problems with p-pops because she held the mike directly in front of her mouth. This not only hid her mouth, but it made the popping sounds more noticeable. If you are using a hand-held mike, the best place for that is right below your chin — not in front of your mouth. Another method for avoiding p-popping sounds is to use a microphone wind screen. This is a screen that is made of acoustically transparent film, and it often comes with the mike.

Check your room before your program. Make sure that the temperature is appropriate and there is plenty of light. If it is too cold or warm, adjust the thermostat. However, remember that the body heat of your audience will warm the room and you want the listeners to be alert. If the room is large and you have only a few people coming, close off the back part of the room with masking tape on the chairs. You can open it up if more people come in.

Be sure to locate controls for the sound system, lights and temperature. Appoint someone to handle any emergencies that can happen while you are speaking. Make sure that there are no lighted sconces behind you. Don't wear jewelry that flashes, name tags or glittery belts.

Know what is happening in the adjacent room. If there is a rock band playing during your presentation, you can rest assured that your speech is going to suffer. The most important axiom is — control your environment.

Be sure that you have set up your room appropriately for the size and type of presentation. For example, for groups of twenty or less, a U-shaped table arrangement works best. This size is ideal for staff departmental meetings, less complex AV presentations, meetings on employee relations issues and training programs.

Classroom-style setting means tables and chairs. This setting reduces the number of people the room will hold. However, if you are speaking to a seminar or workshop, this arrangement allows people to write in their workbooks and lends itself to group participation. It is best to eliminate the center aisle. Ask for the room to be set up so that it has two side aisles instead of a center aisle.

Consider curving rows of chairs slightly so that they all curve in a very broad semicircle rather than straight rows. In fact, chevron or herringbone style lets the participants see one another. For large groups, when you expect little or no participation, you will need an auditorium or theater-style seating with no tables. Room size compared to number of attendees is tremendously important. Remember that if you have too many people crowded into a small room, the chances of confrontation increase. On the other hand, if you have an enormous room with very few people, the group won't feel connected or cohesive and will not participate actively.

Now that you have organized and prepared for your talk and planned the platform mechanics, it's time to explore the actual presentation by looking at specific speech delivery techniques in the introductions, openings and closings. These elements are extremely important. You can have excellent information in the body of your presentation. But if you don't grab the attention of the audience immediately in the beginning and if they don't know what you expect of them at the speech conclusion, you may not achieve the end goal of your speech.

14

As You Speak

Introductions

Whether someone introduces you or you introduce yourself, your introduction can make or break your speech. If you have responsibility for introducing someone else's talk, you need to understand the importance of your task. The introduction is the true beginning of the speech. The audience often makes up its mind about speakers based on how they are introduced. If the introduction is done poorly, it can take a considerable amount of time to regain the momentum lost.

If someone else is introducing you, make sure he understands the importance of using the introduction you supplied to him. You need to go over it with him in detail. Instruct him not to deviate from the introduction unless he knows you well and has a brief personal anecdote he wants to share. Let me give you two examples of how not to be introduced. Afterwards I will point out what went wrong. Then I will describe a proper introduction and its components.

Here is the first example, an introduction of me: "Okay. Can I have your attention . . . Please, people, can I have your . . . is this mike on? Can you hear me? I'd like to let you enjoy yourselves a little longer, but now it's time to introduce our speaker. Normally this would be done by Judy Doakes, but she is in Podunk, Iowa, and how we all envy her! We usually have a big dance after the banquet. This has always turned out to be the hit of the year, but due to recent turndown in business, we've decided to do something a little cheaper — a speaker. So now, let's have the speaker — Patty Berg."

What was wrong? The introducer said nothing about me, nor why I am here at this time and speaking on this subject. He didn't give enough information. He certainly did not set the stage. Finally, to add insult to injury, my introducer got my name wrong.

Here is the second poor introduction:

"Now, it's time for our speaker. Before I introduce the speaker, I have an important announcement to make. As you know, there was an emergency meeting of the Board this morning. Rumors are flying about layoffs due to the stock market crash and subsequent loss of business from eight of our major clients. After a lengthy meeting in which four of our board members resigned and one left due to serious chest pains, it was decided that there must be some layoffs here in River City. I regret to inform you that approximately sixty percent of you will be terminated. However, in order not to dampen the spirit of the Christmas party, we have decided not to reveal who will remain and who will be fired . . . I mean phased out, until after the party tonight. Our speaker tonight is a trainer and a speaker. She will inform and entertain. How about a warm and enthusiastic welcome for Patricia Ball."

Although I was exaggerating to have some fun, this horrible introduction illustrates an important point. One major purpose of an introduction is to set the stage for the actual speech. It is the frame for the picture. It serves as a transition. Make sure your introducer saves negative announcements for another time. They can dampen or even destroy the spirit of the audience.

To summarize, a proper introduction has the following elements:

1. It puts the audience at ease and sets the stage for your speech.
2. It tells why **this** speaker, at **this** time, before **this** audience, on **this** subject.
3. It includes the program title, who you are, what you've done and why you're qualified.
4. It is brief — less than sixty seconds — tactful, friendly and accurate.

5. It has been carefully read and approved by you. The only exception to this is when the introducer is a friend or colleague who can add a warm, personal note.
6. It ends with your name.

Effective Openings

The next major point deals with developing effective openings for your speeches. Remember the purpose of the introduction is to get the listeners' attention, to set the mood and to introduce the topic. The next step is to grab the audience's attention with a great speech opening. Think about some techniques that you have used to begin some of your talks. You *don't* get the listeners' attention by saying, "Good morning! I'm so pleased to be here. What I want to talk to you about today is . . . ." You need to grab them from your first word. Come out punching!

If something unforeseen happens before your presentation, find a way to use it in the opening. Many years ago I was to present a "Dress for Success" program to two hundred male IBM managers in Minneapolis. Early in the morning on the day of my program, I was in my room, "dressing for success." I had not gotten very far. I was wearing a full black slip, but I did not have on any shoes, hosiery, skirt, blouse or makeup. I had not had time to comb my hair yet, which was standing on end as a result of a restless night's sleep. I looked like the Bride of Frankenstein! Room service arrived with my breakfast. I hurriedly looked around for my robe. Drat! I had left it at home. Wrapping a towel around me, I opened the door just enough for the server to slip inside and put the tray on the nearest table. I signed the tab and hurriedly ushered him back through the door.

After eating breakfast, I peeked outside the door into the hallway. It was empty! Holding the door open with my foot, I slid the breakfast tray through and placed it on the hallway floor, outside my room. As luck would have it, the coffee container capsized. I grabbed for it without thinking and, in the process, took my foot that was acting as a door stop away from the door. Suddenly I heard an ominous "click" as the door closed and locked behind me! There I was, alone in the hallway, wearing only a black slip! What to do? I padded bare-foot to the nearest door across the hallway, thinking someone would help me. I knocked. An elderly gentleman with a twin-kle in his eye opened the door. When I saw him, I became flus-tered. I said, "I'm sorry. Wrong room!" He replied, "No, honey. It's the right room. You're just forty years too late!"

Totally flustered, I took the back stairs down three flights. When I looked in the lobby, luck was with me. It was empty with the exception of a woman behind the front desk. I gath-ered up all the dignity I could muster and padded barefoot, black slip and all, to the front desk. I asked for another key to my room, explaining that I had locked myself outside. *As if I had to explain.* The clerk looked at me suspiciously. She said, "Do you have any identification?" Nonplussed, I answered,"Do I *look* like I have any identification? I forgot to wear my dog tags." I finally convinced her to give me a duplicate room key. I went to the elevator, pushed a button and waited for what seemed like an eternity. Finally the elevator arrived. The doors opened. There, like peas in a pod, were 10, three-piece, navy blue-suited IBMers. The man in front was the man who had hired me. He looked at me strangely, turned to the men in the elevator and said, "Gentlemen, this is the speak-er I hired for the 'Dress for Success' program!"

I could have let the incident die right then. Instead, I dis-carded the speech opening that I had planned to use. Later that morning when I began my speech to the two hundred male managers, I said, "How many of you had an opportunity to see me early this morning . . . not fully clothed?" The men who had been in the elevator chuckled. The others looked confused . . . but definitely interested. I then said, "The program for today is called 'Dress for Success.' One of the axioms we are going to explore has to do with not making assumptions about others. So before you make an assumption about what I just said, let me tell you what happened to me." I had them in the palm of my hand! When something happens to you, use it.

Following are a number of examples of openings that will grab attention.

• **Use a startling statement.** In one of my programs on managing a diverse work force, I begin, "By the year 2000, eighty five percent of all new entries into the American work force will be immigrants, women, Asians, Blacks and Hispanics." This statement makes you immediately aware of the near future look of the workplace and why we need to be cognizant of diversity issues.

• **Use humor.** Rather than tell a joke, recount an amusing incident to which the group can relate. Try out the story on friends a few days prior to your speech for its humor rating.

• **Ask questions.** Your questions can be direct or rhetorical. With a direct question, you expect the audience to answer and you ask for a show of hands after each question, acknowledging those who have raised their hands. With a rhetorical question, the audience will not physically respond but will mentally answer the question. In my program on self-esteem and positive attitude called "Create a More Powerful You," I open with this series of questions: "As one of the first things you do in the morning, how many of you look in the mirror? . . . How many of you *avoid* looking in the mirror as long as possible?" *There is a tittering of laughter at this point.* "When you look in that mirror, how many of you look for something negative — a new wrinkle, a gray hair, a blemish or maybe the absence of a hair or two? . . . On the other hand, how many of you get inspired by what you see?" *There is more laughter on this one. Then I ask the last question.* "How many of you look in that mirror and say to yourself and mean it, 'I am a very special person?'" *Very few, if any, raise their hands.* Now comes the kicker. "I believe that every single hand should be raised. It's so important that we feel that we are special. Without a healthy self-esteem and positive attitude, it's difficult, if not impossible, to be a success at anything in life that you attempt." This immediately leads into the subject of my presentation.

• **Refer to the specific occasion or audience.** Here is an introduction from one of my theatrical programs called "A Portrait of the American Woman." "During this celebration of Women's History Month, the Federally Employed Women here are to be commended for taking the time and this occasion to honor these heroines of the past."

• **Refer to yourself.** I once said to a national convention of postmasters, "I too have worked for the post office. I was one of the first female mail carriers." I received a round of applause. "I drove a rural mail route the summer before I started college." This story immediately endeared me to them and made me one of them.

• **Use a human interest story.** The night that I received my CPAE or Council of Peers Award for Excellence — the 'Oscar' of the speaking profession — was one of the most memorable evenings of my life. The story that I told that night about my special dad was referred to earlier in a different context. I am repeating it here with a different slant, because it is an excellent example of a human interest story.

"It was a college speech contest. The judges had narrowed it down to me and a male student. Our final assignment was to rewrite our speeches and present the new versions in a week. That was a hectic week. I also was playing the lead in a play, managing my own dance studio and maintaining a scholarship with a full course load at Washington University. I didn't spend enough time learning the new version of my speech. When I stood in front of the judges, the new speech went right out of my mind! My mind went blank! I couldn't even remember my name! Humiliated, I left the stage.

My dad was in the audience and said, 'It's not important that you've lost the contest. What *is* important is that you look over your speech right now and ask the judges if you can try again.' I went back on stage — the most difficult chore that I have ever had to do — and finished the speech. My dad knew that if I didn't try again, I might always be afraid of public speaking. Thanks, Dad, for your wisdom, love and support."

• **Use a quote.** There are numerous books of quotations on the market. Occasionally a well-known movie will supply you with a usable quote. One line from *Forrest Gump* has great possibilities: "Life is like a box of chocolates. You never know what you are going to get until you dig into one." A manager might say that the next few years of the company's growth will be fraught with the same kind of uncertainty, but the employees still need to dig right in because the rewards can be sweet indeed.

Conclusions

Here are some ways to conclude your speeches with pizazz. Remember to give your audience a final summary before you close your speech. In other words, tell them what you told them. However, don't announce your conclusion by saying things like "In conclusion . . .," "To sum up . . ." or "I have tried to demonstrate . . . ."

• **Tie the conclusion back to the introduction.** This technique wraps your speech into a nice neat package. If you began the presentation with a quotation, find a similar quote to conclude.

• **Close with humor.** As you can see, many of the same devices that I mentioned for the introduction will work for the conclusion. In one of my programs to speakers on presentation skills, I tell the story of Demosthenes, the well-known Greek orator. He practiced elocution each day by filling his mouth with marbles until finally, there were no marbles left. The moral of this story is that you have become a professional speaker when you've lost all your marbles!

• **Close with an inspirational poem or story.** In a persuasive speech, it works well to find a way to tug at the audience's heart strings. One tug is worth a thousand words.

• **Clarify the startling statement you made at the beginning of your speech in light of what you have told your** audience. When I open with "By the year 2000, eighty five percent of all new entries into the American work force will by immigrants, women, Asians, Blacks and Hispanics," I can repeat the quote. Then I close with the statement, "Through the skills outlined in this program, you and your company can use this influx of work force diverse groups to give your company a competitive edge."

• **Use a call to action.** Tell your audience what you want them to do. Be sure to keep the tempo up. Build an energy by increasing its forcefulness. "Don't stay in your homes and become complacent. Register now. Vote in the next election! You can make a difference!"

• **Repeat a phrase, several times, intensifying the delivery each time.** President Lincoln used this technique in "Government *of* the people, *by* the people and *for* the people." The repetition adds power to the message.

• **Challenge your audience.** "Do we have what it takes to put this project over the top?" Place the onus for the activity on the audience. Give them a call to action.

• **Use a historical perspective.** "Joe Jackson believed this when he founded the company, and we have continued in that tradition . . . ." The purpose is to create a metaphor out of a past activity which relates to your desired direction into the future.

• **Give the listeners a choice.** "We can do nothing and slide further behind, or we can . . . ." By using contrasting statements, you emphasize the focus or direction of your message.

Remember, the three most powerful elements of a speech are the introduction, the opening and the conclusion. The introduction gets the audience in the mood and sets the stage for the speech. The opening grabs the audience's attention. The conclusion leaves them in an upbeat frame of mind and motivates them to take action.

We have discussed the organization of your speech. We have explored the mechanics of staging. Now let's examine some techniques that will improve your speech delivery, including vocal, nonverbal skills and audience involvement.

15
Mechanics of Speech Delivery

Maximizing Your Vocal Skills

The goals of the actor are to be natural on stage, to sound conversational and to look extemporaneous. As a speaker, you are confronted with similar challenges.

Memorize the beginning and conclusion of your speech because of their importance, but rehearse them so thoroughly that the delivery sounds natural. Learn to extemporaneously explore the remaining points as you go through your presentation.

Use the "umm humm" technique to lower the pitch of voice described in an earlier chapter. Work in your lower vocal range. If you want to emphasize a word or phrase, drop your pitch down a notch or two for what you want to highlight rather than rising up the scale. *Whisper* a poignant line. Whispering catches the listeners' attention. Use short sentences and active voice. Keep your voice interesting by varying your pitch. Avoid a monotone delivery. Monotones make any speech dull and boring. Audio tape yourself in rehearsal. If you find your vocal delivery is all at one pitch level, correct the problem by varying your delivery. Practice by reading children's stories out loud in an exaggerated manner. Tape yourself as you read and listen to the tape.

Articulate clearly. One of the most frequent problems I encounter in speakers is the omission of ending consonants in gerunds and participles like *fishin'* or *speakin'*. This lazy pronunciation leaves the audience with the impression of a less-than-polished person — certainly not a straight talker. Practice the following sentences out loud and enunciate the ending consonants with great exaggeration:

Healthy and alert speakers use a wide variety of exercises — walking, lifting, running, swimming and loving.

They do this by leaping, plunging, swelling, writhing and sweating.

Also, watch the t's and ch's. *Over-use* these in rehearsal. Remember Hamlet's advice to the players, "Speak the speech I pray you as I pronounced it to you, *trippingly* on the tongue." When your tongue has great flexibility, you are more likely to use ending consonants with your words.

One common cause of articulation problems is a "frozen upper lip." Put your finger on your upper lip as you speak. If it doesn't move, you have a frozen upper lip. In rehearsal, force yourself to move your upper lip.

If your voice sounds tired, speed up your delivery to give yourself more vocal energy. Communicate enthusiasm, confidence and sincerity to your audience.

Proper breathing habits are essential for successful and effective public speaking, just as they are for singing or acting. Proper breath support won't make you sound like Judith Anderson or Orson Welles, but it will help you sound like the best possible you.

Since the voice is one of the speaker's most valuable tools, train that tool wisely. You can chop down a tree with a dull ax, but if you hone the cutting edge to its finest, you will cut the tree down with much greater control. *Control* is the name of the game.

Most of the faults in speaking voices are due to poor or incorrect breathing or lack of breath control. If you want good voice quality, you must learn good breath control.

How do you control your breath? You do so by controlling the contraction of the muscles around the diaphragm so that the breath is forced out of the chest cavity in a smooth, steady stream. In the past, you may have been told to breathe from the diaphragm. This is inaccurate. The intercostal muscles surrounding the diaphragm do much of the work. According to Dorothy Sarnoff in *Speech Can Change Your Life,* the intercostal muscles are 'the girdle of breath support.' These muscles exert pressure on the diaphragm causing it to push air up your windpipe from your lungs. The air passes through all of your speech apparatus — vocal cords, nasal passages, mouth — and comes out as words. To locate the 'girdle of breath support' and the diaphragm, place the palm of your hand flat on the area about three inches above your navel and at the bottom of your rib cage. Now take a deep breath and exhale slowly. See what happens to that area when you do.

Sarnoff suggests that you imagine a car going up a steep hill. If you don't give it a steady supply of gas, increasing the pressure as the hill gets steeper, the car will slow down, give a few wheezes and gasps and stop. You need a continuous, steady supply of air to keep your voice from "running out of steam." Breath support will make your voice sound strong and vigorous. Lack of proper support will result in a tired, old-sounding voice. A sip of air is all you need to speak a long phrase or sentence. Learn to take "catch" breaths through your mouth. These sips are delicate and quick. Catch breaths require control of the diaphragm muscles. When I first started making audio recordings and voice narrations, one of my biggest problems was that the microphone in the sound studio — a particularly sensitive device — would pick up my heavy breathing sounds. I was taking in huge gulps of air in what should have been silent pauses. It took me a while to learn to take catch breaths. The prerequisite to a clear, supported voice is muscle support, not deep breathing.

An important step in gaining control is learning to relax. Before a speaking engagement, take a deep breath, then exhale as slowly and steadily as possible. Do this several times. Open your mouth and yawn a few times. Yawning can't help but relax you.

Posture is an important consideration. Keep your chest up, stomach in, shoulders relaxed. If you are standing, keep your weight evenly distributed on the balls of the feet. Now slouch forward into poor posture, rounding your shoulders. You can feel what happens to your diaphragm and chest cavity. You can't get a proper supply of air in those cramped quarters.

As an actor, when I want to depict a character who is tired or depressed, I will collapse my diaphragm area, round my shoulders and push my stomach out. My physical appearance changes and my voice sounds tired, listless and weak.

Your voice projects most of your personality. Your voice is your best tool for expressing kindness, anger, fear, confidence, sadness and humor. These feelings can all be found in your voice. Whether you have a deep voice, a high voice or a sexy voice isn't really important. It's how you use it. There's no need to eliminate the accent of your native region or country. Just polish it. A heavy southern accent won't keep you from being an effective communicator unless people have trouble understanding you.

Care of Your Voice

If you don't care for your voice, other people won't care for it either. How do you take care of your voice, particularly if you have a cold? One factor is proper breath support. Without that support, you will be a constant candidate for hoarseness, sore throat and laryngitis. Here are a number of other brief tips:

• **Don't strain your voice.** Do not shout in noisy surroundings. In fact, avoid noisy environments as much as possible. Reduce your volume when you are talking on the phone and avoid screaming.

• **Reduce your overall amount of talking.** Give your voice ten to fifteen minutes rest per hour of talking. Talk one third less in every conversation.

• **When hoarse, drink lots of water.** Drink a glass of water a meal and sip throughout the day. Use a humidifier in your bedroom at night. Avoid breathing through your mouth, although this is hard to do if your nose is congested with a cold.

• **Eliminate all harmful vocal habits.** Throat clearing, chronic laughter, crying, physical grunting due to stress and exercise, voice imitations and impersonations strain your voice.

- **Reduce your intake of caffeine and alcoholic beverages.** Both dry up nasal and speech areas.
- **Don't smoke.**
- **Get enough sleep.**
- **Get the nutrients and calories you need.**
- **Keep a daily log of your vocal activity,** including the date, time, activity and voice-use rating, if you are having a problem with your voice.
- **Talk in the lower registers,** if you are suffering from vocal fatigue or hoarseness.

Developing Powerful Nonverbals

Speakers and actors both create imagery through movement. On the surface there is one kind of communication: the verbal medium of words. Below the surface there is a second way to communicate emotions and feelings, namely nonverbal communication. The surface level is conscious. The second level, the emotional image, must appear unconscious. The audience needs to see feelings and emotions beneath the smooth flow of surface behavior. It's important for the speaker as well as the actor to remember that for every physical action, there is something psychological happening. For the actor, this impulse is called motivation. What is your motivation as a speaker? Is it to inspire? To entertain? To get the audience involved? To impart knowledge? The inner motivation may change from moment to moment, and it will affect how you move and gesture. It can even affect *where* you walk on the stage or platform.

A stage is divided into six parts — downstage right, downstage center, downstage left, upstage right, upstage center and upstage left. These directions are defined by the actor's left and right as she faces the audience. Each section of the stage has meaning. Research shows that each area has different strengths and mood values. No one knows why this is so, but actors are taught these factors very early in their training.

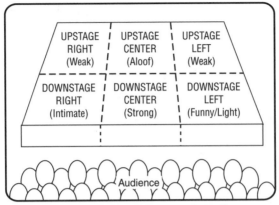

STAGE SECTIONS

The center area of the stage is the strongest, with downstage center being the strongest area of all. Downstage center is the site of strong, intense climactic moments. As a speaker, I reserve this area of the platform for the most powerful points in my message. Upstage center is second in strength, but more aloof in mood value. Downstage right is the third strongest area. It is best for intimate scenes. Save your stories with pathos, the ones that touch the audience, for this segment of the stage. Downstage left is less strong and is often used for lighter moments. Have a fun audience-participation event or tell a humorous story from this area. Upstage right and upstage left are the weakest of the stage areas. In theater, these areas are used for crowd scenes and unimportant characters. As a speaker, I seldom use these areas. These are rough guidelines, not rigid, unbreakable rules. Block your speech, and choose carefully where you move on the platform.

Great speakers are total speakers. They speak from their toes up. Their bodies are alive. They have strong physical presence and energy. Speeches are physical activities, not just mental ones. Can you imagine a good actor with a passive, inexpressive body? When a good actor steps on stage, there is an almost tangible charge of energy. Critics call it *electricity*. As a speaker, you want to communicate to your audience that you care enough about them to stay excitingly awake.

You may recall our discussion in an earlier chapter about rising/approaching actions and sinking/withdrawing actions. Rising energy is associated with a vigorous person; downward movement is related to the tired or sick. Be vigorous. When you walk to the platform, let your head move delicately forward and up, away from your body, allowing your body to follow. Walk purposefully with wide strides, lifting your rib cage and focusing on where you want to go on the platform. Plant yourself with your feet spread apart approximately one foot and your weight evenly distributed on both feet.

Here is an important rule to remember: "You cannot *not* communicate!" Even when you are silent, you are communicating something. Each of us is a kind of transmitter that cannot be shut off. The fact that we are all constantly sending nonverbal clues is important. It means we have a constant source of information about ourselves and our audiences. It also means we can't hide or fake feelings from the platform. A thought passes through our unconscious. Our faces, extremities and torsos unconsciously react to that thought. The body language action starts *before* the idea is expressed verbally or even consciously thought. Our timing needs to be in sync with our actions and verbal expressions.

Gestures to Avoid

There are five major categories of gestures that weaken platform performance:

• **Incomplete gestures** — For a gesture to have full strength and impact, it must begin in the lower torso area with a lift of the body or a withdrawal of the body, depending on the emotion you are conveying. The movement should continue to full extension of your arms and legs. When the torso is left out of a gesture and movement occurs only in the limbs, the gesture seems stingy, half-hearted, lacking in energy and incomplete.

The torso contains vital organs that are intimately associated with emotions and consequently with the impulses of the body to move. The backbone functions as a main spring for all of the larger and more expressive movements of the body. It gives vitality and energy to the movement of the secondary agents — the legs, arms and head. To see how involving your torso in movements adds energy, wave your arm without moving your torso. Then, wave your arm with a movement beginning from the lower back area and continuing with a total follow-through as in tennis or golf. Notice the difference in energy? In vitality?

• **Gestures above the neckline** — Except for an occasional exception, gestures above the neckline lack power. They are often used to primp or preen. Touching the glasses, fixing the hair or scratching the nose are signs of nervousness. Exceptions to this rule include arms raised in a V shape in response to applause or larger expansive gestures geared to a huge audience.

• **Incongruent gestures** — To be credible, your words and gestures need to convey the same meaning. Your body language must be congruent with what you say. If the messages are conflicting, you body will leak tell-tale signals and sabotage you. When words and body are speaking different languages, people believe the body, rather than the words.

Suppose you are talking about how terrific you feel and about the importance of maintaining a positive attitude. However, your arms are crossed, your fists are clenched and your facial expression is solemn. People will read your mixed messages and will not take your words seriously.

• **Powerless gestures** — Many gestures send negative or powerless messages to your audience. The gesture of putting both hands in your pockets is often read nonverbally as secretive or critical. It is a sign of nondisclosure. If light reflects off your glasses and the audience can't see your eyes, they might read nonverbally that you are hiding something. Wear non-glare glasses or contact lenses.

Pointing a finger at the audience can have a hostile, belligerent meaning. Avoid nervous gestures — tugging at the skirt or trousers or any general self-repair. Don't look over the heads of the audience at a spot at the back of the auditorium. They will know you are not looking at them. Avoid clenched fists. Avoid the fig-leaf gesture with the hands crossed in a V over the crotch area. This posture makes you appear self-conscious. Hands on hips are often perceived as aggressive or defiant.

• **Gestures inappropriate to audience size** — Some speakers' gestures are the same size whether they are playing to a group of ten or a crowd of five hundred. Make your gestures fit the size of your audience. For a small group or for television, your movements need to be the same as if you were talking to someone face-to-face. As audience size gets larger, gestures need to be slower and bigger than life, bolder — more definite, more purposeful. Your gestures need to be clear to the person in the last row.

Straight-Talk Body Language

We've explored gestures that rob you of power. Now let's examine gestures that add to your authority on the platform.

• **Plant your feet.** Remember to stand with feet apart and your weight evenly distributed. You then nonverbally say, "I can stand on my own two feet."

• **Keep your palms visible.** Hands held forward with palms up convey sincerity and openness.

• **Put your hands behind your back on occasion.** This gesture can demonstrate hidden power. It is called parade rest in the military and is often used by authority figures. It also hides shaking of the hands. However, use parade rest sparingly. If the hands are hidden for too long, the audience becomes suspicious.

• **Grasp the lectern with both hands,** while standing behind it. Demonstrating your ownership of the lectern is good for power. Again, use this gesture sparingly. A lectern also acts as a barrier between you and the audience. It is best to learn to use the rest of the stage and move from behind the lectern. This is called "working naked" on the platform.

- **Make eye contact.** Look at a specific audience member, finish your thought, hold eye contact for a moment and then go to another audience member. Your audience will feel that you are speaking directly to each individual in the audience. This one-on-one connection is powerful.
- **Be the same on the platform as in person.** On the platform, you want to be the same as you are in real life, only a little bit bigger and louder.

Involving the Audience

Much of the success of a speech depends on drawing audience participation. One of the most effective ways to involve your listeners is through a question-and-answer period.

The simplest participation occurs when you **ask questions of your audience that require their responses.** For example, ask for a show of hands. Be sure to recognize the show of hands. Say something like "I see most of you agree" or "Only a few hands raised."

Make the questions easy. Nothing is more embarrassing to people than not being able to answer questions because they are too difficult. One typical easy question is "What do you expect to get out of this presentation?" Move close to the audience to make it harder for them to avoid participating.

You can also **ask the audience to define a word.** In my "Winning With Power Communications" program, I tell the audience, "Power is an interesting word because it has both positive and negative meanings. Think of a single word definition of what the word 'power' means to you. Please raise your hand and when I point to you, just shout it out." I give the attendees these instructions. Then I pause. The pause may seem like an eternity to the audience, but I wait for a response. People are afraid of silence. They rush to fill in the space.

When you **ask questions that require responses from individual members of the audience** you get a variety of answers. The solutions coming from the audience are more memorable than they would be if you simply told them. Always agree with someone who volunteers an answer. You can simply say, "Excellent" or "Absolutely." If someone says something that is totally opposed to what you are saying, you can answer, "That's an interesting thought. I'm sure there are others who would agree with you." Be sure to thank people after they ask a question.

In addition to asking questions that require responses from your audience, **give the audience an opportunity to ask their questions or make comments.** When you ask the audience for their comments, there is often a piggyback effect. Questions or responses from one person inspire questions from another. If your audience balks at asking questions, prompt them. Say, "Here are the kinds of things I'm looking for. I'll give the first two examples, and then I'd like to hear from you." I get a lot of participation with this technique. No question is a bad one.

Tell the audience at the beginning of your program when you will be accepting questions. State what you expect from your listeners so that they can prepare and know what to expect. Remember, you are in control. If you want to wait until the end of your presentation to take questions, tell your audience so. If you are going to take questions throughout the program, tell your audience to feel free to ask questions as they arise. Always *repeat* the question, particularly in a large group. The people at the back may not have heard it. Don't evade or make up an answer. If you do not have an answer, say, "I don't have the answer to that question." You could also offer the participant the option of "I don't have the answer, but that is an interesting question. I'll be happy to find out for you and let you know, if you'll give me your name and address after the program."

To encourage people to participate, **give a small gift to the first person who responds.** I frequently give away audio cassettes of my speeches. Renowned speaker Joel Weldon offers tin cans that have the words "I can" written on them.

Learn to relax. Banter with the audience. If something funny happens and the audience laughs, laugh with them. If you have a good comeback, don't be afraid to use it.

Speakers have many options available to them for getting the audience involved. Here are some general tips to use to encourage audience participation.

Use ice breakers. "How many of you were sent by your boss? . . . How many of you were sent by your secretary? . . . How many of you had the whole office take up a collection to send you? . . . How many of you wouldn't raise your hand no matter what?" Obviously, a couple of those questions are ludicrous and will generate some laughter. This loosens up your audience which is what you want to accomplish.

Play terrific up-beat walk-in music right before your introduction. However, be sure to get permission from ASCAP for specific musical selections. Check with the meeting planner to see if the organization has blanket permission. You can also have music written for you.

Music puts people in the mood for fun. In fact, if you want to start the music playing when you come on stage, you can ask the audience to stand and clap to the music. Clapping is a great energizer. If the group has been sitting for a while, this is a good way to stretch their muscles.

Do not read your speech. You want to create excitement. There needs to be excitement in your voice. If you aren't excited, you can't expect your audience to be. Exaggerate what you normally do, particularly at the beginning of the program. Speak a little faster than normal. Keep your voice pitched low so that you don't rise into the higher registers.

Use your acting skills. Re-enact what you are describing to your audience so that you paint a mental picture for them. When you describe "running up the stairs," actually do some foot movement as if you are running, exhausted and out of breath.

Never make fun of anyone in your audience. That is the quickest way to cut off any future possible participation. I once heard a speaker say to a person who was leaving the room, "We know where you're going." Never embarrass an audience member.

Some miscellaneous techniques to use are as follows:

Give handouts with fill-in-the-blank segments to your audience. Be careful that there are not too many blanks. If the audience spends the entire time writing, they will miss some of what you are saying and they won't enjoy the presentation as much. Use an outline form so that the handout is easy to follow. To help listeners to follow along, you might even say, "In the middle of page three of your handout, we're talking about . . . ."

Fill out some three-by-five cards in advance that relate to your topic. Pass these cards to various attendees. When the time comes, have each audience member with a card volunteer to read what is on the card.

At the outset of your program have people take a few minutes to meet as many people around them as possible. Have them stand up, shake hands and tell their names and occupations. This is a great energizer.

Have the audience stand up and do some simple stretching and relaxation exercises. If your presentation occurs mid-afternoon, people will be at their blood-sugar nadir.

If you want to form discussion groups, have the people at the various tables turn to the table behind them, turn their chairs to that table and form groups of no less than four and no more than six people. To assign leaders to the discussion groups, one fun method is to have everybody hold a single finger in the air and then count together, "One . . . Two . . . Three!" On the count of three, each person drops the pointing finger toward the table member he chooses to be the leader. It's fun and is a quick way to assign a leader to a group.

Facing a Hostile Audience

In most instances, your audience will be in a positive frame of mind. They want you to succeed. However, there might be occasions when the audience is required to be present. The message they are receiving may be unpopular. If you face a hostile audience:

• **Prepare yourself.** Know your material inside and out so that you can answer their questions with expertise.

• **Know your audience.** Know their values, opinions and their knowledge level so that you don't speak down to them.

• **Understand that you are not the target of their hostility.**

• **Give yourself the right:**
  • To be treated with respect
  • To express your views accurately
  • To resist manipulation
  • To say you don't know the answer

• **Breathe correctly and be physically centered.** Nonverbal behavior affects verbal behavior. If you can be relaxed and non-fearful in your body language and posture, you will be better able to handle hostile questions.

• **Be prepared to listen and empathize.** It's amazing how these skills can neutralize hostility.

You have developed your vocal skills for maximum power. You have learned to use your body so that it communicates meaningfully. You are comfortable in front of an audience. You are able to interact successfully with them, getting them to ask questions and participate fully.

You are almost ready for Opening Night! Successful straight talking requires that you explore one final, vital area — dress and image — the costuming for the stage of life.

16
Dress Rehearsal - Image and Dress

In theater, the final rehearsals are called "dress rehearsals." Actors wear their costumes and make-up to convey their character to the audience. As we tread through the stage of life, our *costumes* communicate vast amounts of information to others. Now we will explore image and dress for the straight talker.

Image

People have difficulty coming up with a clear-cut definition of image when asked to define the term. Yet they have no problem telling you who, in their opinion, has or does not have a professional image. Their judgment is based on an overall assessment of the person. Although important, dress is only one factor that determines professional image. The verbal, vocal, nonverbal and behavioral straight-talking skills explored in the preceding chapters are all a part of one's overall image.

A professional image comes from projecting personal power that gets respect. Your image depends on the level of competence you present to others. The level of competence you present depends on your sense of being valued and self-empowered. Since you build your image from the inside out, self-esteem and the other internal tools of the powerful that were examined in the earlier chapters are particularly important.

In the chapter on self-esteem, *choice* was a vitally important word. We make choices every moment that we live. We choose to wear one outfit over another. We choose our words, phrases and intonations. We decide on one behavior and discard another.

To create the ultimate straight-talk image, you need to show a level of competency. If you know and recognize your own value and power, others will perceive you as being valuable. Another tool that helps others understand your value is self-control. You make choices every day about how much self-control you are going to exhibit. I am sure you know people who often choose to be angry. When they are strident, screaming and out of control, what do you think about their level of competency?

An image of competence needs to be consistent. It must be the same today, tomorrow and the day after. You can be angry, but you need to be in control of that anger. Don't allow your voice to become strident. Watch your body language. Avoid clenched fists, frowns and tense neck and facial muscles. Don't use inflammatory words.

You need to look in control on the outside, in spite of what you may be experiencing on the inside — whether that be anger, butterflies in your stomach, depression or even a physical problem. A number of years ago I attended a National Speakers Association Workshop in Atlanta. It was to be a busy time for me. I had appearances in front of the crowd of six hundred on each of the three days of the meeting.

For comfort, I had traveled in jeans, planning on changing into business attire when I got to the hotel. I arrived in Atlanta mid-morning; my luggage did not. My first presentation that day was not until 3:00 p.m., but I had to attend meetings up until that time. I had no time to shop for new clothes. Not wanting to appear in front of this prestigious audience in jeans, I was bemoaning my situation during lunch with friends — a speaker and his spouse. The wife, Sara, asked me, "What size do you wear, what designers do you prefer and what colors do you like?"

She took a fifty-dollar, round-trip taxi ride to Neiman Marcus and returned to my hotel room with several thousand dollars worth of clothes! I was to choose what I liked and return the rest when my luggage was found. What a friend! The only difficulty was the hosiery. You may recall that I am almost six feet tall. That's a lot of stretching to ask of any pair of hose. When I put on the pair that Sara had purchased, the crotch was a good two inches below where it needed to be and the waistband was three or four inches below my natural waist, making a dent in the biggest part of my hips. Luckily the long suit jacket hid this problem. However, when I tried to walk, I felt like a rubber band. The hosiery would stretch and spring back, causing me to walk with little mincing steps. It was almost time for my presentation, so I went on stage wearing the ill-fitting hose. No one could tell from the outside of my outfit that I was in such disarray underneath my clothes. I kept my image of self-control.

What should your image be? Your image, both professional and personal, should be comprised of two elements:

- It should be a genuine expression of who you really are.
- It should be appropriate to your situation, environment and culture.

Let's examine these characteristics — first, a genuine expression of who you really are. While you no doubt believe that you know yourself very well, you don't. You would be shocked to learn what messages others are receiving from you — messages you never intended to send. Think for a moment of a time when someone said to you, "You look really angry. Have I said something to make you mad at me?" You may have replied with genuine surprise, "Angry? Why would you say that? I'm not angry at all." You were angry, and you looked it. For some reason, you were unaware of your own feelings and how obvious they were to the other person. You were giving conflicting and incongruent messages.

If something like that has ever happened to you, two things were taking place:

- You didn't know yourself very well at that moment.
- You had no idea what kinds of messages you were sending.

I have said this before in previous chapters, but it is so important that it bears repeating. **EVERYTHING ABOUT YOU NEEDS TO CONVEY CONSISTENT MESSAGES.** If you send inconsistent messages, people will believe what they see and discard what you tell them.

Secondly, your image should be appropriate to your situation, environment and culture. What do we mean by that? Do you remember President Carter's casual dress during his first fireside chat? Later in his Presidency, when the country needed a sense of confidence in its leadership, he delivered his messages from behind his desk in the oval office dressed more formally in a dark suit, white shirt and tie. The latter dress communicated leadership and confidence, not informality and approachability. How will a corporate president be viewed by his directors if he attends the board meeting dressed in the same sweater and blue jeans that he wears to the plant employees' meeting Saturday morning?

If you are a Wall Street stockbroker, an appropriate choice for work would be a conservative suit. If you are an art director in an advertising agency or working in a *glamour* industry, you would be wise to avoid conservative clothing in favor of more *with-it* gear. You need to dress appropriately for the situation, environment and culture. If you don't want to risk giving false signals, dress to convey the image you want to convey.

The First Impression

You may have heard the well-worn phrase, "You never get a second chance to make a first impression." This statement is trite; it is also true. People make up their minds about you in the first thirty seconds that they see you. Eighty percent of what you communicate is visual, so you have already said a great deal about yourself before you say hello. Therefore, business dressing is an important communication skill. You create a communication bridge with the way you dress. The visual impression you make strongly influences people. If that first impression is wrong, it will cost you great effort to correct those mixed messages.

I have said that eighty percent of what you communicate is visual. What **do** you communicate? There are nine decisions that people make about you when you walk into a room:

- Current economic status
- Current educational status
- Trustworthiness, moral character
- Current social position
- Level of sophistication
- Level of success
- Economic heritage, background
- Social heritage, background
- Educational heritage, background

If there are any inconsistencies in what people see and hear, they will believe what they **see** every time. Perhaps you have heard the phrase, "What you are speaks so loudly, I can't hear what you say!"

Image is not phony. It is simply the impression you make on other people when they see you. You form similar impressions of them every day. You meet someone new, and you take a fast, almost unconscious inventory of that person. You may think, "She's a class act," or "I don't know why, but I don't trust this guy." A thousand clues bombard you simultaneously, and your first impression is set in an instant.

The impression people form when they meet you may be precisely the one you want them to have, or it may be quite the opposite of what you intended. In a business setting that impression could make the difference between making a winning presentation to the CEO or having your proposal turned down. Remember the last time you felt like a million dollars? Think about the kind of service you received that day when you walked into a store or restaurant, the upbeat way people treated you and the way everything seemed to fall into place for you. Whether you realized it or not, you were projecting a strong, positive image to the world, an image that conveyed these messages: "I look great, I feel great and I'm loaded with confidence!" Everyone you met picked up those messages and responded to them in an equally upbeat way. Were you projecting a phony image? Not at all. In fact, it was an extremely accurate one. You were feeling positive and confident and everything about you broadcast those feelings, just as you broadcast other feelings on your bad days — the ones when your spirits are low and you look and feel more like two cents than a million dollars.

You nonverbally shout feelings with the expression on your face, with the tone of your voice, with the way you stand or walk, with your eyes, clothes and body language. In fact, whether you talk or not, most of the time you are broadcasting information to anyone who comes within twenty feet of you. You project an image of yourself to others, whenever there is anyone around to see it. That image is a reflection of you and what is going on inside of you. If you feel you could conquer the world, it shows. If you feel the world might well conquer you, that shows too. When you walk into a room, someone takes your measure in one sweeping glance, beginning at the top and swooping down to your feet. First, your form — your size and shape — alerts people. Your form sends its own messages, even if they are not always accurate. Tall people are viewed as leaders; overweight people are often seen as lazy or slow. Of course these are stereotypes, but nonetheless they exist. If you are taller than the other person, you may intimidate him. If you are shorter you may be overlooked. You may think your form is a given, but you can change the **perception** of that body. The set of your shoulders communicates degrees of power. By standing erect, lifting your rib cage, sucking in your stomach and setting your shoulders back, you exude energy, which, in turn, can create a perception of influence and power.

If you are short, think of yourself as a small giant and you can be one. According to research, being short sometimes creates image problems, but there are some steps you can take that will help. Short people need to consider spending more money on their clothes, even if that means buying fewer of them. Looking crisp and put together adds to a person's ability to project power. Check yourself several times a day. Make sure that every hair is in place, shoes are shined and your clothes look well-tailored and fit beautifully. Dressing immaculately helps to create an illusion of power.

A person taking an inventory sees your face next. If you are hiding your face with dark glasses or long bangs, you may give the impression that you are hiding something else. Perhaps you are even dishonest. Eye contact is powerful. Two other dramatic steps you can make that will cost you nothing are smiling and relaxing. A smile says you are congenial, pleasant and happy to be there. Your smile needs to be appropriate, not continual. Obviously, when you are first meeting someone, you hope to convey to her the image that you are glad to be there and want to become acquainted with her. In a first meeting a tense face tells someone you are uptight. Take a deep breath, calm down and loosen your muscles. Your face will follow suit.

The sweeping inventory ends at your feet. Scuffed and dirty, unrepaired shoes or saggy, baggy, drooping socks or hose are considered character defects. Nonverbally, they show a lack of concern for detail and an inability to follow through. In a business setting, short socks or white socks for men are not acceptable. For women, closed-toe pumps are best. Your shoes need to cover your feet.

Dress

Just as costumes communicate the character an actor plays, the clothes we wear define us in many different ways — as being conformists, being non-conformists, possessing poor self-images, dressing against the grain, or being part of a power symbolism. The way you dress makes a statement about you, and it is sometimes the opposite of the statement you want to make. We have been taught all our lives never to "judge a book by its cover." We all do just that. We make value judgements based on people's appearance.

We are all very aware of the importance of our appearance — even self-conscious about it. During a formal dinner, Lady Astor remarked to her neighbor that she considered men to be more conceited than women. Noticing that her comment had been heard around the table, she continued in a loud voice, "It's a pity that the most intelligent and learned men attach least importance to the way they dress. Why, right at this table the most cultivated man is wearing the most clumsily knotted tie!" The words had no sooner left her lips than every man in the room surreptitiously reached up to adjust his tie.

Dress is a difficult area to discuss in any great detail because the rules change so rapidly from year to year. American businesses are becoming more informal than ever before. The rules of dress are relaxing. The main rule to consider is **the power of sameness.** People trust people who look like them, dress like them and act like them. They may question people who look different from them. They may perceive the other as not **one of them.** In business, people don't usually dress for their own comfort or self-expression. They dress as a sign of respect for others and the position they hold. That is how you create a bond of commonality between them. Play it safe. Dress down, understate and emulate those around you to establish your position and identity.

Many years ago my husband Ken paid a visit to a customer in a small town in California, a state known for its casual way of life. Because no one had forewarned him, he dressed in a suit, shirt and tie. Ken was standing across the desk from the customer, when suddenly the customer reached in the top drawer of the desk and pulled out something shiny. In one quick movement he crossed around the desk and cut my husband's expensive tie off near the knot! Anyone who had ever visited that office before knows that no one wears ties in this small California town. All of the townspeople feel strongly about it.

A group of New York advertising agency people pitching the Apple Computer account in California left their conservative suits at home and dressed down in sports jackets for the presentation. They landed the account. Dress appropriately for the situation, environment and culture in which you are functioning.

Here are some specifics regarding business dress for success. As the work culture changes, some of these rules will change as well. What is applicable to the workplace today may not be tomorrow.

Business Dress for Women

Women who want to be taken seriously and who **want** to succeed need to dress in a way that says, "I am important. I am a business professional." One of the reasons some women don't succeed is because they don't look like they **want** to succeed. According to studies in John T. Molloy's *The Woman's Dress for Success Book,* the business uniform for a woman that says loudly and clearly, "I am a business professional," is a good skirted suit, preferably in dark or neutral shades, with a contrasting blouse. One interesting finding is that, as women become more confident in high positions in the work place and as there are more of them in those positions, conservative dresses with jackets are acceptable business dress. Moderate shoulder pads are wonderful for helping a woman achieve a look of authority.

Conservative jewelry — and very little of it — is in order. It should not make "noise" but rather be a focal point — a quality jewelry piece that makes a simple statement.

The floppy bow or tie at the neck is no longer a necessity for businesswomen. You will see all kinds of necklines in blouses in a work setting. The only rule is to avoid a too low-cut blouse. Decollete not only gives a sex-symbol message, but the lower the cut, the more vulnerable a woman is. Cleavage makes you an ornament, not a businesswoman. A leather briefcase is a good investment. If you can do without a handbag, ditch it. If you can't, a small shoulder strap bag or clutch is now acceptable with your briefcase. Invest in a good pen, one that you don't have to dig in a purse to find. Take care that even your business card reflects the image you want people to have of you. Learn to carry your business card case in a suit pocket. This saves you the awkwardness of digging through your purse to find a card.

Levels of Dress for Women

Clothing is a system, with each stage conveying competence, authority and confidence. Here are the levels of dress for women:

• **Level One** is a dark business suit. This epitomizes the person-in-charge in an established business setting like money fields. Strong colors like cobalt blue, fuchsia and violet — vivid, clean colors, not pastels — also fit into this category. A jacket paired with a business dress is acceptable at some upper levels.

• **Level Two** is a business dress with clean colors and a simple line — no ruffles, lace or cute touches. It is still a good idea to wear a jacket for meetings. Solid color pants suits are acceptable in many traditional but creative settings. However, pastels or tight pants send a powerless or sexy message. Without a jacket, this look is too casual for the straight talker.

• **Level Three** is a skirt and tailored shirt or blouse. Although this can sometimes work well, it does not carry the same authority as the previous levels.

• **Level Four** is a skirt and blouse with a more feminine touch like ruffles or pastel colors. The look does not carry as much power as the other levels. Pants with a tailored shirt can have a stronger effect if done well. Pants with a solid blouse deliver a softer promise of ability and competency.

• **Level Five** is the most casual level of clothes for a work setting, acceptable for casual days or a less formal setting. Play clothes like shorts and culottes fit into this category. Take note: Extremely short shorts worn at a company picnic are a hard image to shake at business meetings.

Women now continue to work throughout their pregnancies. Maternity clothes should not broadcast how sweet and cute you are but rather that you are a business professional.

Levels of Dress for Men

Just as there are five levels of dress for women, we might think about the same for men.

• **Level One** is a dark business suit, preferably pinstriped navy blue, black or charcoal gray, with a conservative tie. The ultimate business shoe is the wing tip. A white shirt nonverbally symbolizes honesty. Red in the tie is a great touch; it's a powerful color. Silk ties are preferable. No polyester anything at this level. An excellent touch is a thin, high-quality watch. Fit of clothing is important; it denotes status. All five elements of your suit, shirt, tie, shoes and socks need to be expertly coordinated to achieve the total effect. The wrong shirt or tie can destroy the effect of a perfect suit.

• **Level Two** allows lighter suit colors like light gray or beige. Contrasting shirts in pastels are worn at this level.

• **Level Three** is a sport coat or blazer with contrasting slacks. The tie is still worn with this look.

• **Level Four** is less formal. At this level the tie is discarded, allowing for a simple sports shirt and slacks.

• **Level Five** is the most casual level. On casual days in the workplace this might mean khaki slacks and colorful shirts. Shorts are appropriate in few instances during work hours, perhaps for a company picnic or outing.

Miscellaneous Dress Pointers

The jacket is the ultimate symbol of authority for both sexes. Notice how a man will put on his jacket when someone of status enters his office or when he is going to another office for a meeting, even if he is not going outside.

Dress for the income and position you want, not the one you have. This may mean fewer but more expensive clothes. According to Molloy, "Executives who wear expensive clothes recognize those who don't."

Straight-talk colors that connote power are red, white, navy blue and black. Brown was once considered a color that lacked authority. Since President Reagan wore brown suits so frequently, the color brown has come to carry more power.

Fabrics that carry a powerful image are wools and gabardines. Suedes and velvets, while expensive fabrics, are too soft for a power image.

We have explored the final touches for the straight talker — image and dress. We've learned how to present an image that demonstrates a level of self-control, competency and consistency. We've discussed that all-important first impression. We've looked at our life *costumes* — the various levels of dress and what each level communicates.

In the same way an actor learns his or her part, our own stage of life has taken us through the read-through, the working rehearsal and the final dress rehearsal. If you have read and absorbed everything to this point, you are now ready for opening night!

17

The Grand Opening - Putting It All Together

When great actors are thoroughly enmeshed in their parts they **become** their characters to such a degree that it is difficult to separate them from their roles. Think of the multiple roles played by Dustin Hoffman, Meryl Streep and Lawrence Olivier. You become convinced that they are the characters they are depicting on the stage or screen. Their craft is so hidden that their acting comes across as natural, spontaneous and easy. Yet these actors work hour after hour on small movements and vocal intonations until they are as they want them. Then they practice to perfection, so that the gesture or inflection becomes a part of them.

As you play your various roles on the stage of life, you should do the same. The secret to becoming an excellent straight talker is to practice so diligently each and every day that straight talk becomes second nature to you. Your attempts to persuade others will seem effortless. You will always seem to make the correct straight-talk choices.

There is a high steep cliff in Acapulco, Mexico, from which divers dive into a narrow ocean inlet. Split-second timing is required. Being off in timing for only a matter of seconds can mean hitting the rocks or sides of the cliff instead of the narrow section of waterway. Yet the graceful divers make the dive look effortless.

My husband Ken and I witnessed a tragedy there one night long ago. Because it looks so simple, young boys from the near-by villages are always attempting these dives. That night a young villager dove to his death as we watched, horrified. In this instance, the seasoned divers had made it look *too* easy.

Picture the Olympic skaters who glide gracefully on the ice, floating from one difficult maneuver to another, smiling in fun all the while. Yet the daily grind of practice, practice, practice never lets up for them as they continually hone their craft.

Power Communication

Real power comes from within. Power is an attitude, not a series of words. Your posture, gestures and expressions must flow freely and naturally from yourself. Believing in yourself gives you a positive emotional surge.

Powers From Within

Straight talkers work hard to understand themselves and to help others to know them. They project honesty, vulnerability and strength all at once. In the concentric circles representing our self-images, as the area of self-knowledge grows in size, the other images — the bare, concealed, oblivious and obscure — become smaller. We, and others, learn more about ourselves.

Straight talkers develop the following powerful internal behavior styles.

• Straight talkers are persistent and determined. They deliver on their promises and commitments.

• Straight talkers are visionaries who continually set new and higher goals for themselves.

• Straight talkers look to the future. They analyze trends and anticipate changes.

• Straight talkers read voraciously and continue to learn.

• Straight talkers are not afraid to take risks.

• Straight talkers work hard to keep negatives from influencing them. They speak and think mainly in positives.

• Straight talkers are assertive. They are able to walk the tightrope between passivity and aggressiveness.

Choice is the most important word in the English lexicon. We make choices each and every day: how we feel about ourselves, our level of self-esteem and our self-worth. Great actors possess a healthy self-esteem, a necessary ingredient for convincing an audience. As you apply for a job, go for an interview, present a proposal or make a speech, you must begin by convincing yourself. Use only positive "self-talk."

Straight-Talk Behavioral Tools

Listening actively is one of the most important habits you can develop. It will help you in everything you attempt in life. Nothing is more flattering than a person who validates others by listening to them. Learn to ask questions and adopt appropriate nonverbal listening modes.

Understanding the ways in which each gender communicates is a powerful tool for getting along with others. This knowledge will help to eliminate misunderstandings between the sexes. Your knowledge will help you to recognize and respect the differing communication styles. It will help you to develop effective straight-talk skills.

A sense of humor is a wondrous attribute. Studies indicate that this is one of the traits that managers seek in people when hiring. Humor allows you to persuade others, to defuse criticism and to convey authority. Learn to *think funny* and look for the humor that is always around you.

Learn and use the verbal tools of the straight talker. Powerful communicators consistently use direct statements. They make their words matter. They understand the power of silence and know when to pause and to listen. They avoid *weasel* and *waffle* words, speech qualifiers, empty superlatives and put-down statements.

Straight talkers know and master all aspects of nonverbal communication. They understand the nuances of paralingual messages. They practice reading other people's body language. Then they test their hypotheses for correct interpretations. They learn to make their bodies work *for* them by rehearsing positive nonverbal body language cues. Straight talkers understand spatial relationships or *proxemics* — the importance of where you stand, move and sit in relation to others.

Unique situations like conducting meetings, giving presentations or handling conflicts require a special set of communication skills. If it is *your* meeting, you can get noticed in a positive way by distributing a comprehensive agenda, setting your room appropriately for maximum impact and having professional visual aids. You need to keep the meeting running smoothly and on time and allow all participants an opportunity to have a say.

If *you* are a participant, keep in mind the following three straight-talk principles for being persuasive in meetings.

• **Timing** — Before contributing your opinion, consider all the issues being raised. Decide on your top priorities and focus on them. The best time to voice your opinion is at the beginning or the end of the meeting. Your ideas are more likely to be remembered, and you will appear more persuasive.

• **Tone** — Be clear and assertive. Disclaimers like "I don't really have much data to back this up" or "You may not agree with this but . . ." detract from your power.

• **Tact** — Acknowledge the value or truth of what others say, and then continue with your own point of view. "What you say is true, Sue. We have been sloppy in that area. But I still maintain . . . ." Using this method, you help the other person to save face.

Conflict situations require another specific set of straight-talking skills. Learn to use the powerful responses to confront criticism and remember the five modes of conflict resolution, as well as the appropriate occasion for each conflict-resolution use. Strive to collaborate whenever possible.

Generally, as you rise up the success ladder in business, you will be required to make more and more presentations. Learning to make an effective pitch is an important business skill to hone. Review the various factors of an excellent presentation. Use relaxation techniques and humor to dispel speech anxiety. Organize your speeches, and use visual aids and audience participation to enhance your effectiveness. Deliver your presentation with impact and ease. The ability to speak well will earmark you as a powerful straight talker.

Maintaining a professional image at all times is vital to straight talk. How you *costume* yourself for your life role helps determine how others view you. The choices you make every day in your clothes, hair style and posture make an impression on others. Make sure that, in all cases, you project the impression that you want to project.

As you can see, straight talk is so much more than words alone. It is how you talk, how you move, how you dress, what you mean by what you say, where you sit. If you rehearse and perfect straight-talk skills, you will communicate with confidence and clarity. When the curtain rises on *your* opening night, consider Shakespeare, and instead of being "a poor player that struts and frets his hour upon the stage and then is heard no more," *Macbeth,* you will be a "well grace'd actor, leaving the stage," *Richard II.*